Jane Barlow

Irish Idylls

Jane Barlow

Irish Idylls

ISBN/EAN: 9783744709484

Printed in Europe, USA, Canada, Australia, Japan

Cover: Foto ©Thomas Meinert / pixelio.de

More available books at **www.hansebooks.com**

Irish Idylls

By
JANE BARLOW

New York
Dodd, Mead and Company
1898

NOTE.

THE illustrations in the present edition of *Irish Idylls* are the result of a trip made to the Connemara boglands of western Ireland, for the express purpose of securing material that should be absolutely true to the descriptions in the text. I have tried to make the pictures faithful transcripts of nature and life as they really are amid the sombre bogs that are the predominant features of that part of the Irish west coast. It is doubtful if in any civilised country there are people whose homes and lives are more forlorn than those of these Connemarese folk; and it is no wonder that Miss Barlow's portrayal of them in their out-of-the-world villages, in their petty strifes, their pinching poverty, their loves, their disappointments, and their triumphs, has attracted wide attention. Here is the whole gamut of human nature, in spite of the forbidding environment; and it touches a responsive chord in every sympathetic heart, no matter how differently situated.

The traveller in Connemara cannot but be impressed with the fact that Miss Barlow preserves the atmosphere of the region and the sentiment of the life she describes to a rare degree; and it is believed that pictures and text together will give as vivid and interesting a view of peasant thought and ways and surroundings as has ever been published.

CLIFTON JOHNSON.

PREFACE.

IN Lisconnel, and other such places, we have a saying that *there are plenty of things besides turf to be found in a bog.* This little book attempts to record some of these things, including, I hope, a proportion of that "human nature" which a certain humourist has declared to exist in considerable quantities among our species. I hope, too, that the phases of it pictured here may have some special interest for American readers, to whose shores the wild boglands of Connaught send so many a forlorn voyager "over oceans of say." They will perhaps care to glance at his old home, and learn the reasons why he leaves it, which seem to lie very obviously on the surface, and the reasons, less immediately apparent, why his neighbours bide behind. It is indeed the fact of those emigrants that chiefly encourages me to believe there may be room and a welcome across the Atlantic for this one emigrant more.

JANE BARLOW.

RAHENY,
   County Dublin, May, 1893.

CONTENTS.

CHAPTER I.
	PAGE
LISCONNEL	1

CHAPTER II.
| A WINDFALL ... ... | 14 |

CHAPTER III.
| ONE TOO MANY ... ... | 40 |

CHAPTER IV.
| A WET DAY ... ... | 76 |

CHAPTER V.
| GOT THE BETTER OF ... ... | 107 |

CHAPTER VI.
| HERSELF ... ... | 143 |

CONTENTS.

CHAPTER VII.

	PAGE
THUNDER IN THE AIR	164

CHAPTER VIII.

BETWEEN TWO LADY-DAYS	204

CHAPTER IX.

BACKWARDS AND FORWARDS	242

CHAPTER X.

COMING AND GOING, ...	285

CHAPTER I

LISCONNEL.

THERE is a great deal of room all round and about Lisconnel. That is, perhaps, what strikes one most upon arriving in sight of its half-score cabins, though the impression may have been growing all along the seven Irish miles from Duffclane. They could not well be measured on a lonelier road through a wilder bogland. The broad level spreads away and away to the horizon, before and behind, and on either hand of you, very sombrely hued, yet less black-avised than more frequented bogs. For the turf has been cut only in a few insignificant patches; so that its darkness lies hidden under an ancient coverlid, sad-coloured, indeed, but not sharply incongruous with sunshine. Heath, rushes, furze, ling, and the like, have woven it thickly, their various tints merging, for the most part, into one uniform brown, with a few rusty streaks in it, as if the weather-beaten fell of some huge primæval beast were stretched smoothly over the flat plain. Here and there, however, the monochrome will be broken: a white gleam comes from a tract where the breeze is deftly unfurling the silky bog-cotton tufts on a thousand elfin distaffs; or a rich glow, crimson and dusky purple dashed with gold, betokens the profuse mingling of furze and heather blooms; or a sunbeam, glinting across some little grassy *esker*, strikes out a strangely jewel-like flash of transparent green, such as may be seen in young moss.

But these are very rare, unusually rare, in the bogland between Duffclane and Lisconnel. The picture you bring away with you on most days of the year is of this wide brown floor, sweeping on to meet the distant sky-line. Whenever your eyes follow it to the southward, you become aware of faint, finely-limned shapes that haunt it, looming up on its borders, much less substantial, apparently, in fabric than so many spirals of blue turf smoke. They are big *bens*, the remotest of them numbered, it may be, among those twelve towering Connemarese peaks, which in Saxon speech have dwindled into Pins. Any country body met on the way would point out which dim wraith is Ben Bawn or Ben Nephin. But I hardly care to identify them; they seem as if they were looking in out of another world to remind us how far off it is.

As for the road, it has determined that the wayfarer shall never lose his sense of the great solitudes through which it is leading him. In all its length it has scarcely half a dozen yards of any kind of fence—wall, bushes, or even the humblest ledge of bank. It runs quite flush with the bog on either side, sometimes edged by a narrow strip of the short fine sward, where, if the district were inhabited, geese would waddle and graze; but there is nothing to shut out the limitless expanses of earth and sky. Travelling on it, a man may learn that a broad hat-brim is not an altogether despicable screen between his imagination and the insistence of an importunate infinity.

One autumn season a hapless Neapolitan organ-grinder strayed somehow into these regions, with his monkey clinging round his neck. It is a long time ago, but a generation afterwards people remembered the lost, scared look in the eyes of man and beast. They both fell ill and died in the Town down beyond, as if, poor souls, they had not the heart to keep alive in the vast, murky, sunless world that had been revealed to them. And to this day you are pointed out the Frenchman's grave—for a foreigner here is always a Frenchman—in the churchyard beside the lough.

The road, one of Scotch Nimmo's making, is generally drawn straight enough, though now and again it swerves considerably to avoid a wet piece of bog, and, straight or winding, its course may be traced for miles ahead, a streak across the landscape, not strongly marked, except in very dry weather, when there is white dust on it, yet distinct as a crease in the palm of your hand. One peculiarity of such a road is that you never come upon anybody sitting close beside it. For since in damp climates people habitually avoid seating themselves on the unsophisticated surface of the earth, and since neither stone dyke nor hedgerow bank offers a handy perch, it follows that any one who happens to be keeping an eye on geese or goats, or setting down a heavy creel, or waiting for the loan of a lift, must find a resting-place on some boulder or boss more or less off the beaten track. Hence the passer-by is occasionally given the time of day, or the top of the morning, in a startling shout, which proceeds from some figure whose presence he had not surmised ; as the bog, like a converse chameleon, often has the property of subduing superimposed objects to its own vague tints.

This, however, makes little difference on the Lisconnel road, so few people pass along it. At the Duffclane end a donkey may now and then be met carrying a tall pyramid of chocolate-brown turf-sods, based on two pendent panniers, between which his large head bobs patiently, while beneath the load his slender, tottering legs take quick staccato steps, each scarcely the length of one of his own ears; or an old woman comes by with a creel projecting quaintly under her dark-blue cloak; or a girl saunters barefooted after a single file of gabbling geese, knitting a long grey stocking as she goes, and never seeming to lift her eyes from the twinkle of her needles. But after you have gone a short way the chances are that you will meet nothing more civilised and conversable than wild birds and very large gnats, until you come in sight of Lisconnel.

Just before that, the road starts abruptly, as if it had suddenly taken fright at its own loneliness, and dips down a steepish slope, but quickly pulls itself up, finding that escape is impossible. The hill, whose spur it has thus crossed, is very insignificant, only a knoll-like *knockawn*, prolonged on the left hand as a low ridge, soon dwindling into a mere bank, and imperceptibly ceasing from the face of the resurgent bog. Yet it probably fixed the site of Lisconnel, because it offered some protection from the full sweep of the west wind, and because its boulder-strewn slopes, and a narrow strip at their foot, have a covering of poor light soil in which potatoes can be set. Such advantages seldom recur within a radius of several miles. For when I spoke of the spaciousness of Lisconnel I did not mean that there is much room in it for you or me, or anybody who must needs have "a bit of lan'" to live on. The craggy ridge is surmounted by a few weather-worn thorn bushes, and one ash tree, so strongly warped to the eastward that a glance at it on the stillest day creates an impression of blasts blowing roughly. Also, after the manner of trees thus situated, it seems to draw down and diffuse the very spirit of the desolate surrounding solitudes. The cabins themselves look somehow as if they felt its spell, and were huddling together for company. Three in a row on one side of the road, a couple fast by on the other—not exactly facing them, because of a swampy patch—two more a few paces further on, with "Ody Rafferty's" and "the widow M'Gurk's," which stand "a trifle back o' the road" up the hill-slopes, climbing down to join the group. That is all Lisconnel, unless we count in the O'Driscolls' old dwelling, whose roof has long since top-dressed a neighbouring field, and whose walls are in some places peered over by the nettles.

Cabin walls in Lisconnel are built of rough stones with no mortar, and not mud enough to preclude a great deal of unscientific ventilation, which, maybe, has its advantages, dearly paid for through many a shivering night. All its roofs are thatched, but none of them with straw, which is too scarce for such a use. Rushes serve instead, not quite satisfactorily, being neither so warm nor so durable, nor even so picturesque, for their pale grey-green looks crude and cold, and the weather only bleaches it into a more colourless drab, when straw would be mellowly golden and russet. A thick fringe of stones must hang along the eaves, or roof and rafters would part company the first time the wind got a fair undergrip of the thatch. Stones, as any one can see, are superabundant in Lisconnel, but ropes are not so easily come by, and therefore a block is sometimes just dumped down on the roof. When that is done, the rainwater gathers round it, and the thatch begins to rot. The largest window in Lisconnel measures not less than nine inches square, and is glazed with a whole pane of real glass, through which strangely distorted glimpses of the outer world may be had; but opaquer substitutes are not at all exceptional; and in every case the door practically shuts out the daylight, unless the wall-chinks gape abnorma ly wide. These habitations have been, when possible, purposely built on pieces of ground where the rock lies bare in flat ledges, or hidden by a mere film of soil; for the supply cf by any means tillable land is so strictly limited, that not a yard of it may be diverted from the accommodation of "the crops"—poor little things. Moreover, the living rock underfoot forms a convenient ready-made flooring, barring a slight unevenness here and there. In the Sheridans' cabin, for instance, a well-defined central elevation divides their room into a northern and a southern slope, and acts as a water-shed during wet weather.

The immediate surroundings of a Lisconnel cabin are not generally much more untidy than any other part of the bog, but this is perhaps due less to the neatness of its occupants than to the scantiness of their materials for making a litter. Similarly, if little waste, as a rule, goes on at Lisconnel, it may be not from thrift, but of necessity. It is right to mention these facts, yet I hope it will appear that not all the virtues practised there are thus to be explained away. A turf-stack looms darkly somewhere close by each door, and when newly "saved," and therefore at its largest, looks like a solidified shadow of the little house. A big black pot sits so customarily over the threshold, pried into hopefully by disappointed fowls, that when it goes indoors the landscape seems unfinished. Against one end-wall huddles a small stone-shed, which can be thatched promiscuously with a few armfuls of withered potato-stalks, if there are any creatures to keep in it. Oftenest it is empty. The live stock of Lisconnel never exceeds half a dozen goats, as many pigs, and a few "chuckens"; and in bad seasons these vanish as speedily as swallows after an October frost. Once the place owned a donkey, but that came to grief, as I may explain further on.

Therefore the hopes and cares of the inhabitants centre mainly in the little grey-dyked fields which make a plaid pattern on the hillside, and along a meagre belt beneath; and this renders it the more regretable that their most prolific and certain crop should be such an unremunerative one. Stones upon stones, scattered broadcast by some malignant Hundred-handed, and perennially working up through the thin soil, in mockery of ten-fingered attempts to collect and keep them under. Those loosely-built boundary walls, which intersect so frequently that the bit of land looks as if a coarsely-meshed net had been flung over it, fail utterly to exhaust the supply. In each diminutive field a great cairn of them is painfully piled up, as big, sometimes, as the cabin to which it belongs, and still the husbandman comes on them at every turn; they trip him up as he stumps between his struggling potato-drills, and grin maliciously at him through the sparse, stunted tangle of his storm-tossed oats. Everywhere he can read, written large, an answer to his demand for bread.

The people of Lisconnel have, it is true, a few other minor resources by which to supplement deficiencies, and tide over periods of stress, rent-days, for example, and blights, and "buryin's." When harvest begins, some of the men tramp off with their sickles round their necks, and get jobs in districts where farms are on a larger scale. They do not go to any great distance, for lack of means and enterprise. And the women knit stockings of the harsh-feeling, dark yarn, hanks of which are hung in festoons over the counter of Corr's shop in the Town away beyond Duffclane. This might become the source of quite a handsome revenue, swelling to whole shillings a-week, since a moderate knitter can finish a long stocking from knee to toe in a day; only that the demand for the article is sluggish, and Mr. Corr can give but small and intermittent orders. "Och no, Mrs. Quigley, I've no call for any such a thing these times at all. Sure, I've a couple of pair of the last I took from you hangin' up yet; and by the same token it's much if them little slieveens of moths haven't eat them into thread-lace on me agin now." At which hearing Mrs. Quigley trails away with her old market-basket, and one new disappointment the more. There is yet another method by which pennies are sometimes turned at Lisconnel, but it might seem hardly fair to mention that in a general review of the inhabitants' pursuits. Most of them take no more active part in it than that of "not letting on," which is, after all, a neighbourly attitude, often expedient for us to adopt, whatever our position in society.

So, by hook or by crook, Lisconnel holds together from year to year, with no particular prospect of changes; though it would be safe enough to prophesy that should any occur, they will tend towards the falling in of derelict roofs, and the growth of weeds round deserted hearthstones and crumbling walls. You may see the ground-plan of more considerable places than Lisconnel sketched in this forlorn fashion on many a townland thereabouts. It would not be easy to judge from their aspect to-day how long it is since these cabins were newly built, for they look as if they might have grown up contemporaneously with the weather-fending *knockawn* itself, which is clearly impossible. As a matter of fact, seventy years ago none of them existed. However, soon after that they were run up rather hurriedly, and tenanted by some people who, it is said, came thither reluctantly from a more southerly district, where there are now flourishing grass farms. Whatever their private views on the matter may have been, the destiny of these persons was evidently appropriate enough, for Lisconnel is poor and insignificant, and we are told that the gods ever bring like to like. So the new-comers settled down, where some of their descendants remain to this day.

Indeed until within a few months since, one of the original colonists was still living there, a very old body, much given to reminiscences of the home she had left so long ago that she should have remembered it well. But hardly credible were the statements she made about that countryside, with its meadows where the grass stood higher than the tallest rushes out on the bog yonder, and its potato and barley fields you could scarce see from one end to the other of, they were that sizeable; where there were cows and calves, and firkins of butter, let alone lashins and lavins of skim-milk and whey; and where a big potful of oatmeal stirabout was set down for the breakfast every morning, and as often as not there would be a bit of bacon frying for the dinner on a Sunday. She expected it to be believed that she had lived in a house containing three rooms, one of them with a boarded floor, and as corroborative evidence would point to a battered pewter pint mug, which used to hang on a dresser in that apartment. Most of her hearers accepted this as perfectly conclusive testimony. "And I mind a little black hin I had of me own, wid a top-knot on her. Many's the handful of dirty oats I've thrown the cratur. Sure it's not to the hins we'd be throwin' them, childer, these times, if we had them whativer."

But now that she is gone, these traditions will share the fate of all such legendary lore, growing stranger and wilder and more obviously unhistorical with the lapse of time, until they add just a tinge of wistfulness to conjectures about the receded past. "Four cows, bedad, and a bit of a cart drivin' in to the market—well tubbe sure, but it's the quare ould romancin' she had out of her." Whereas Lisconnel stands here in the light of common day, a hard fact with no fantastic myths to embellish or disprove it.

CHAPTER II.

A WINDFALL.

THE widow M'Gurk has managed her own farm of more than half an acre ever since her husband's death, which took place one spring several years ago, just when he was about to get in his seed potatoes. They weighed very much on his mind during his last hours, for he gravely doubted the success of his wife's unsupervised operations, and how was she going to live at all if the crop failed on her? She tried to pacify him by assuring him that the ground was frozen as hard as bullets, and all the men in Connaught couldn't work a stroke if they were outside in the field; but he was not deceived, and would have got up if he had been able to stand on his feet. Pitaties were all that day the burden of so much discourse as is possible to any one with double pneumonia, which his neighbours diagnosed as "a quare wakeness on his chest"; but about sunsetting Father Rooney, summoned by Mad Bell, rode up on his old cream-coloured pony, and he gave the sick man some consolation.

"Well, well, M'Gurk," he said, "she'll have good neighbours to assist her any way, and she'll do grandly, with the blessing of God. When I was coming along just now, I think I noticed one of the boys getting across the dyke into your bit of field there, with a graip over his shoulder, like as if he was about doing a job for you."

M'Gurk sought to verify this cheering news by looking through the span of window, which was near his head, but as it happened to be glazed with the lid of a tin biscuit-canister he could not do so, and had to take the statement on trust. However he said, "Glory be," and thenceforward seemed "aisier like" until the small hours next morning, when he grew easier still.

Mrs. M'Gurk's subsequent career, though not exactly *grand*, even for Lisconnel, has in a measure, at least, justified Father Rooney's prognostications. The people have been ready enough to do good turns for a neighbour who takes high social rank as a lone widdy, without chick or child belongin' to her in this world, the crathur. But her own peculiarities sometimes ran counter to their kind intentions. She was not a native of that country side, and had travelled to it along a path declining from better days, most grievous for her to tread, as she had the proud and independent spirit through which the steps of those coming down in the world are vexed with a thousand thorns. After more than half a lifetime, her heart still turned to the place where she had spent her long young years of comparative prosperity, before her father "got drinking." She could not bring herself to accept the lower level as a permanent one, or to abandon an absurdly palpable fiction, according to which she was recognised as well-to-do and in want of nobody's help. Hence, whenever she was known to be in straits, the neighbours had to consider not only their own ways and means, generally a puzzling question, but also susceptibilities on the widow's part, which often proved no less embarrassing and restrictive. A little too much outspokenness, a little over-precipitancy in taking the hint which she was sometimes lothfully constrained to let fall, would convert any attempted relief into grounds of dire offence.

It would not do, for example, to come bouncing in, as Judy Ryan did one evening, bringing a pailful of potatoes, culled cautiously, though in no grudging mood, from a slender store—if Judy threw back a handful at the last moment, it was not her will consented—and saying: "Och sure, Mrs. M'Gurk, I've heard you're run out o' pitaties;

why, it's starved you must be, woman alive, cliver and clane. Here's an odd few I've brought you in th'ould bucket, and they'd be more, on'y we're gettin' shortish ourselves." Judy was immediately informed, with a lamentable disregard of truth, that Mrs. M'Gurk had more pitaties than she could use in a month of Sundays, and was at the same time given to understand, with an impolite absence of circumlocution, that the sooner she removed herself and her ould bucket, the better it would be. After which the Pat Ryans and the widow M'Gurk were not on speaking terms for many a long day. Then, on another occasion, she gloomily dug her steep potato-patch all over again from top to bottom, and in consequence had her potatoes a good fortnight late, whereby half of them rotted in a spell of very wet weather, which occurred before they were fit to lift, simply because Hugh Quigley had finished trenching the ground for them without consulting her, thinking that since she seemed whiles troubled with the rheumatics, forby not being altogether so soople as she was, she would deem it a pleasant surprise to find the task unbeknownst taken off her hands.

Incidents such as these led Lisconnel to opine that the widow M'Gurk was "as conthráry as the two inds of a rapin-hook," and their tendency was, not unnaturally, to diminish her friends' zeal up on her behalf. Yet she never so far alienated their sympathies but that she found some of them ready to stand by her at a pinch, and, as they said, "humour her the best way they could."

Perhaps Mrs. Kilfoyle, the old woman who remembered impossible things, was most successful in this respect; which need not be wondered at, since people regarded her as a person who possessed more gifts than a turn for romancing. These were at times summed up in a statement that she had a way with her. The way which she commonly used in her delicate transactions with the widow M'Gurk was to borrow the loan from her of a jug or a mug. What she could want with one it would have been difficult to conjecture plausibly, for she had an assortment of them, much more numerous than any imaginable emergencies could demand, ranged upon her own smoke-blackened shelves. Small articles of coarse crockery would seem to be the one thing in which Lisconnel is sometimes superfluous. However, the fact is that Mrs. Kilfoyle ever and anon toiled up the rush-tussocked slope to Mrs. M'Gurk's abode on the hillside—which she certainly would not have done for nothing, being old, and, though a light weight, less nimble of foot than of wit—with no ostensible purpose other than to negotiate such a loan. It is true that on these occasions she was apt to be struck by a sudden thought just as she took leave.

"Well, I must be shankin' off wid oneself, Mrs. M'Gurk, and thank you kindly, ma'am. Sure it's troublin' you I am too often."

"Not at all, not at all," from Mrs. M'Gurk, whose gaunt head rose two inches higher with the consciousness of conferring a favour—"don't think to be mentionin' it, Mrs. Kilfoyle ; you're as welcome as the light o' day to any sticks of things I've got."

"I suppose now, ma'am, you couldn't be takin' a couple o' stone o' praties off of us? Ours do be keepin' that badly, we can't use them quick enough, and you could be payin' us back when the new ones come in, accordin' as was convanient. If you would, I'd send one o' the childer up wid them as soon as I git home. Sorra the trouble in it at all, and thank you kindly, Mrs. M'Gurk, and good evenin' to you, ma'am." Then, trotting down the hill: "I'll bid the lads to be stirrin' themselves. Niver a bit the cratur's after gittin' this day."

Or it might be : "Good evenin', then, Mrs. M'Gurk, and I'll be careful wid your jug. I was thinkin', be the way, you maybe wouldn't object to the lads lavin' you up a few creels of turf now our stack's finished buildin', just to keep them quite, for it's beyond themselves they git entirely, if they're not at some job. They do have their mother distracted wid their divilments, the little spalpeens"

I believe the widow was never known to take offence at any of these after-thoughts, though I am not sure that she did not now and then dimly surmise a stratagem, which she would have resented fiercely had the contriver been anybody else than this little old woman with her white hair like carded bog-cotton, and a sweet high-piping voice like a small chicken's. But even the other neighbours sometimes managed things adroitly, for Lisconnel is not deficient in tact when it takes time to consider. Still, that tug-of-war between pride and penury could not fail to produce harassing incidents, and the widow M'Gurk swallowed many an ungrudgingly bestowed morsel with bitter feelings of reluctance, which rather more or less magnanimity would have spared her.

But one day she found herself elevated above these mortifications by a little wave of affluence, which swelled up suddenly under her feet. It was a still November morning, with a smooth leaden sky, and wisps of paler mist hardly moving on the sombre face of the bog in the distance; not a morning that seemed to promise anything out of the common, yet it brought a letter to the widow M'Gurk. A letter is almost as infrequent an occurrence in Lisconnel as a burglary in a village of average liveliness, and it usually gets there by circuitous and dilatory modes of conveyance, for which the postal regulations are not responsible.

But the contents of Mrs. M'Gurk's blue envelope were fully as astonishing as its appearance had been. They consisted of a money-order accompanied by a document which explained that this was the share accruing to her from the divided estate of some unknown kinsman, who had died, possessed, as was apparent, of property, in Connecticut, U.S.A. And the money-order was for the amount of *fifteen shillings*.

Do not suppose that Mrs. M'Gurk ascertained these things at a glance, as we might read a paragraph in a newspaper; the deciphering of them proved a stiff task for a more knowledgable person than herself—though, mind you, it was a quare piece of print would bother her, or handwriting either, if it was wrote anyways raisonable. Her first impression, in truth, was that she had received some ominous notice or " warnin' " about her rent, which would imply that she stood in imminent danger of being " put out of it," an apprehension prone to haunt the mind of the dweller in Lisconnel; and winged with this mirk-feathered fear she sped down to consult her nearest neighbours, the Kilfoyles. So great was her hurry that Mrs. Brian

Kilfoyle, rinsing a pot outside their door, remarked to her mother-in-law within :

" Here's the widdy M'Gurk leppin' down the hill like an ould spancelled goat. Be the powers she was narely on her head that time over a wisp of bent-grass. It's much if she's not after scaldin' her hand wid the kettle, for she seems to have got a bit o' white rag on it."

As neither of them could enlighten or reassure her, Brian was shouted for from his adjacent digging, and even he had to sit for a considerable time on the dyke, with the paper spread down in front of him between two broad thumbs, and with a little breeze blowing through his red beard, before he solved the problem. A small crowd had assembled to hear the result, and was properly impressed by the magnitude of the riches which had flowed into Lisconnel. People are generally loth to be in any way baulked of a strong sensation, and so when Mrs. Sheridan said, after prolonged calculatory mutterings, " Fifteen shillin's — sure that's somethin' short of a pound, isn't it now ? " there was a disposition to resent the remark, albeit she really spoke with no wish to belittle, but merely from a habit of estimating things negatively.

" It's more than her half-year's rent, so it is, anyhow, whativer it may be short of," said Pat Ryan sententiously.

"May the divil dance upon the rint," rejoined his brother Tim, "but I'm wishin' you good luck along wid your disthribited fortune, Mrs. M'Gurk."

Public sentiment was on the whole with Tim. Of course if this phenomenal influx of wealth had confined itself less exclusively to a single channel, satisfaction would have been livelier; pennies jingling in your own pocket ring more silverly than shillings in that of your neighbour, and will do so until coins may bear the date of the millennium. Still, the widow's legacy was a popular measure in Lisconnel, and for the time being created among its inhabitants a strong feeling in favour of Fortune's administration of affairs. Their motives, however, were not purely disinterested, because some of them, more especially the women and girls, would for several ensuing weeks retain an irrational conviction that the probabilities of such a letter coming to their own address had been materially heightened. Only by degrees would these illogical persons cease to experience a faint twinge of disappointment when some casual Pat or Mick, returning from the Town, appeared, as might have been expected, empty-handed. It was so easy now to imagine some one again bawling along the road: "Where's Mrs. So-and-so? Sure there's a letter for her they gave me down beyant."

There were a few exceptions to this prevalence

of generous sympathy. I fear that Mrs. Quigley cannot be acquitted of an attempt to dull an envious pang by rubbing the edge off Mrs. M'Gurk's joy, when she said, after a critical survey of the flimsy paper-scrap in which it was at present enfolded: "Well now, *I'd* liefer ha' had the money down straight, or at all ivints one of them blue-and-white pattron, wid the plain black figures. I've heard tell there does be ivery manner of botheration sometimes afore you can git that sort ped—if you iver git it at all."

Mrs. M'Gurk's face fell as rapidly as a barometer in a hurricane, but before it had time to lengthen more than an inch or so: "Divil the botheration," Brian said. "Herself below at the office 'll just sling the amount at you out of her little windy-box, same as if it was a penn'orth of brown sugar over the counter at Corr's. They might be axin' you to put your name to somethin', but sure any ould scrawm 'll do, and they'll settle it up themselves inside. That's all the trouble's in it."

"Och well, they'll be takin' something off of it for sartin'," persisted Mrs. Quigley, reduced to a but paltry and meagre solace; "they're niver for payin' one the full amount of anythin'. Pennies they'll be takin' off."

But Brian said with confidence: "I question will they. And at all ivints a pinny or so's but a trifle here or there. It's yourself 'ud be countin' the spillins when they were pourin' you out a sup o' drink."

So Mrs. Quigley returned, out of humour, to her morning's occupation, which happened to be minding a small baby, patching an old red woollen petticoat with bits of an older blay calico shirt, wishing that the rheumatiz hadn't got such a hould on her right elbow, and wondering by what manner of manes they could contrive to use only the full of the big pot of potatoes daily, when every other potato was bad in the middle, while Mrs. M'Gurk, her faith in her windfall not appreciably shaken, resumed possession of her postal-order, now imprinted blackly with many unofficial stamps.

When the Æschylean Hermês said that Prométheus would not be tolerable if he were prosperous, he voiced a sentiment which most of us have felt at times, though we may never have expressed it so frankly, and which appears rather melancholy and rather grotesque, if one considers it deeply enough. Not that this remark has any special application to the widow M'Gurk, whatever may have been the case with regard to the pioneer philanthropist. Two or three of her neighbours, it is true, did suspect her of seeming "sot up like" by her accession of wealth. But this was merely their imagination. She really was not unduly uplifted, being indeed one of the people in whom a sudden shock of good-luck awakens a keen and compunctious sense of their neighbours' less happy circumstances. When this half remorseful feeling is retrospective in its action, linking itself with memories of those who can be no longer touched by any freak of fortune, it serves as a very effectual safeguard against over-elation. And that is not at all an uncommon experience among the dwellers in places like Lisconnel.

The widow M'Gurk, then, bore her fifteen shillings meekly, and even listened with patience to the conflicting advice which her neighbours liberally gave her on the urgent question of their investment. Four shillings must go "body and bones" to pay off a long-standing account at Corr's—that was one fixed point; but with respect to laying out the remainder of the sum there were as many minds as there were women in Lisconnel, and rather more. On the whole she seemed most inclined to adopt the suggestion offered by old Mrs. Kilfoyle.

"If I was in your coat, Mrs. M'Gurk," she said, "I've a great notion I'd be gittin' meself three or four stone, or maybe half a barrel, of male—oatenmale, I mane, ma'am, not the yella Injin thrash, that's fitter for pigs than human craturs—God forgive me for sayin' so. That 'ud come expinsive

on you, ma'am, I know ; but then 'twould put you
over the worst of the winter grand. Sure there's
nothin' more delightful of a perishin' night than a
sup of oatmale gruel wid a taste o' sour milk
through it—nothin' so iligant, unless it might be a
hot cup o' tay."

Nobody believed Peter Sheridan when he alleged
that if the money were his, he'd just slip it away
somewhere safe, and have it ready to hand towards
the Lady-Day rent. Such unnatural prudence
could be supposed in no one when actually brought
to the test. "It was aisy talkin', and he himself
niver before the world wid a thruppinny bit."

Be that as it may, Mrs. M'Gurk had long before
sunset planned a shopping expedition to the Town
for the very next day ; and it was arranged that
the widow Doyne's Stacey should accompany her,
and help her with her load, which people understood would consist mainly of a heavy meal-bag.
An early start was necessary, for daylight had
shrunk nearly to its shortest measure, and the
Town lies a good step beyond even far-off Duffclane, which, scarcely surpassing Lisconnel in size,
and making no better attempt at a shop than a
cabin with two loaves filling one window, and half
a dozen shrivelled oranges and a glass of sugarsticks enriching the other, gives little scope for the
operations of the capitalist. If you live at Lis-

connel, it is convenient to understand that "down below" means Duffclane, and "down beyant," Ballybrosna, pre-eminently the Town.

There were still thin fiery lines quivering low down on the rim of the ashen-grey eastern sky, and to the westward the shadow of a great dark wing still seemed to brood over the bog, when Mrs. M'Gurk, wearing a hooded cloak, borrowed from Mrs. Sheridan, and bearing a battered osier-basket with a cord handle, loaned by Big Anne, stood ready equipped for her journey. Before she could start, however, she had to make a round of calls upon her acquaintances to inquire whether she could do e'er a thing for them down beyant. This is a long-established social observance, which to omit would have been a grave breach of etiquette; yet, like other social observances, it sometimes becomes rather trying. On the present occasion one might almost have fancied a touch of irony in the polite question. There were so many things she could have done for them if—but there was much virtue in that "if." More just then than usual, for the harvest had been indifferent, and an early spell of cold weather had brought keenly home to the inhabitants of Lisconnel the fact that they stood upon the verge of the long winter. And the people were afraid of it. In the face of those white starving days and black perishing nights they durst not break into their queer little hoards of pence—corners of "hankerchers," or high-hung jugs, or even chinks in the wall—any more than they would have opened their door with an unmetaphorical wolf howling expectantly somewhere fast by. So the widow M'Gurk received only few and trivial commissions: a penn'orth of housewife thread, a couple of farthing match-boxes, and the like. Mrs. Quigley was on the point of bespeaking half a stone of meal, but drew back at the last moment, and resolved to do with potatoes, though her husband, who had begun to scent stirabout for breakfast, looked cast down as he tramped off with his graip. And Mrs. Pat Ryan knew that her children were expecting a penny among them to send for sugarsticks, so she told them angrily to quit out of that from under her feet and be minding the goat. For at such times the heart of the head of affairs has to be hardened, and the process often incidentally gives a rough edge to the temper.

The last people Mrs. M'Gurk called upon were the Mick Ryans. Old Mick, who had long been past his work, and indeed "past himself entirely," as his neighbours put it, was seated on the dyke near the door, waiting till "they were a bit redded up inside," and thinking vaguely that the wind felt cold. His smoke-dried, furrowed face had hardly more expression in it than the little potato patch that sloped up behind him ; but all at once a gleam came into his eyes, and he said very alertly :

"And is it to the Town ye're goin', ma'am ?"

"Ah, well now, father, what 'ud you be after at all?" said Mrs. Mick, his daughter-in-law, uneasily ; for old Ryan was fumbling in his pockets, where in bygone days there used sometimes to be pennies, but where there never were any now.

"Tobaccy," he said, after a pause, and fumbled on.

"Whethen now, goodness grant me patience, what talk have you about tobaccy these times, man alive?" said Mrs. Mick, with slightly threadbare good-humour. "Where'd you be gittin' a notion of tobaccy? Sure Mrs. M'Gurk"—here signalling with a gutta-percha grimace to her visitor for corroboration—"won't be settin' fut within miles of a tobaccy-shop. She's just goin' after a bag o' male. And Himself might be gittin' you a bit comin' on the New Year. Didn't he bring you a grand twist on'y last Lady Day?"

The old man, partly discouraged by the fruitlessness of his researches in his pocket, and partly by the haziness of the prospect held out to him, seemed to let the idea drop, and his face became nearly as vacant a tract as before, with perhaps a shadow on the furrows. And his unmarried daughter, who had also been groping in her pocket but had found nothing to the purpose there, said, under her breath, "The crathur"—two words, which in Lisconnel so often sum up one's judgment upon a neighbour's character and condition.

The widow M'Gurk and Stacey Doyne could not be expected home much before dark, and nobody began to look out for them until quite one o'clock. The ridge of the knockawn behind the widow's cabin commands an ample stretch of the road in both directions, and from that point of vantage there is generally some one on the lookout, most likely for a mere pastime, though watchers there have been sorely in earnest. But the probable proceedings of the two travellers, the various stages of their journey, and all the circumstances connected therewith, furnished unusually abundant material for discussion about the doors and beneath the thatch of Lisconnel all through this quiet November day, not otherwise rich in incident, as nothing more noteworthy occurred than a slight difference of opinion between Mrs. Quigley and Judy Ryan respecting some hens, and an acute yet transitory excitement roused when Mrs. Sheridan's two-year-old Joe was almost swept over the black edge of a bog-hole by the trailing tether-rope of an unruly goat. Neighbours meeting were at no loss for a remark when they could say: " They'll be better than half-ways there by now," or "I wonder what Corr 'll be chargin' her the stone for the male," or "I'm after axin' her to try was there a chanst of anybody wantin' me couple of speckletty pullets. They've given over layin' on me, and I've scarce a bit o' feedin' for them up here at all; when they smell our pitaties boiled, they're in after them like aigles, fit to swally them out o' the pot."

As time wore on, these speculations began to take a gloomy tone, for Mrs. M'Gurk was much later returning than had been anticipated, which naturally suggested some mishap. They might have lost the money-order, that was the favourite hypothesis; or maybe the people at the post-office —Mrs. Quigley reverted, but now without malign intent, to her original theory—would have nothing to say to it good or bad. About five o'clock, when it was quite dark, a gossoon at the Mick Ryans' supposed, with a grin, that they might "ha' met somethin' quare comin' by Classon's Boreen." Whereupon Mrs. Mick, sitting in the dusky background, might have been seen to bless herself hurriedly, while Sally Sheridan, who stood near the open door, edged several steps further into the room: for the place mentioned is an ill-reputed bit of road. And the next time the rising wind came round the hill with a hoot and a keen, all the women started and said: "Och! the Laws bless us, what was that?"

At last, just as Mrs. Doyne was pointing out how easily one of them might have happened to put her foot in a hole in the dark, and break the leg of her, the same way that O'Hanlon's son did a twelvemonth since, bringing back a heifer from the fair, and he lying out on the roadside all night, and the baste trapesed off home with herself as contented as you please—hailing shouts, which softened into a gabbling hum at a closer range, put an end to all such surmises.

Mrs. M'Gurk's shopping had been done on liberal lines, to judge by the bulging of the basket, which she set down on the first sufficiently flat-topped dyke of Lisconnel, while she took a temporary rest, and her friends skimmed the cream of the day's adventures. The ill-fitting lid covered an interesting miscellany, which the uncertain moonlight made it difficult to inspect and "price" satisfactorily: in Lisconnel no newly-imported article can be contemplated with equanimity until everybody who is qualified to form an opinion has guessed how much it cost. The first parcel that came out was the cause of the expedition's late return, having been accidentally laid down on a counter, and only remembered when Mrs. M'Gurk and her companion were a long mile and a half on their homeward way. But the widow felt that she would have tramped back wearily twice as far rather then have left it behind, when Biddy, old Mick Ryan's daughter, whispered to her: "Sure, he was lookin' out for somethin', in a manner, the whoule day; I knew by the face of him wheniver there would be a fut goin' past the door, though what got such an idee into his head bangs me. But I'll give you me word, this livin' minyit the crathur has a couple o' matches slipped up the sleeve of his ould coat that he axed the loan of from Larry Sheridan this mornin'; belike he——"

"Arrah now, look at the size o' the lump that is," interposed his daughter-in-law; "I'm rae ashamed, bedad. He'd no call to be talkin' oi such things. Faith, ma'am, 'twill ha' stood you in——"

"Whisht then, whisht, you stookawn," protested Mrs. M'Gurk, "and don't go for to be puttin' him out of consait wid his little bit of enjoyment, size or no size."

Meanwhile old Mick sat with the expression of one rapt away in a soothing reverie, and slowly fingered his dark twist of tobaccy, lingering gloatingly over the moist newly-cut end. When Biddy offered to fetch him down his little black pipe, he said, "No begob; I'll just be keepin' the feel of it in me hand for this night." Which he did.

There were other delights in the basket. A bundle of portly brown-and-white sugarsticks made some full-grown people secretly wish that they were children too, and left the children themselves, for the time being, without an unsatisfied wish in the peppermint-scented world. It was on this occasion that a reconciliation between Mrs. M'Gurk and Judy Ryan, who, it may be remembered, had offensively obtruded an offering of potatoes, was cemented—durably, to draw omens from intense adhesiveness—by the number and length of the sticks bestowed upon the youthful Pat Ryans. Then there was a large blue bottle with a red-and-yellow label, which contained a "linyeement" warranted to cure the very worst of rheumatics. This was to be divided between Mrs. Quigley and Peter Sheridan, sufferers of many twinges, who would now command, at any rate, the not despised consolation diffused by strong odours of turpentine and camphorated oil. The only pity was that "such powerful smellin' stuff" should be marked *Poison* so very plainly as to scare any one from trying it "in'ards." And in one parcel was a coarse warm woollen skirt for Stacey, instead of the thin rag in which she had shivered along many a mile that day; while another swelled with the knitting-yarn that Peg Sheridan, who was "lame-futted, and lost widout a bit of work in her hand," had been fretting for time out of mind. But the purchases whence Mrs. M'Gurk herself derived the keenest pleasure were the two dark-purple papered packets which she left at the Kilfoyles' cabin, on her way up to her own; no meagre funnel-shaped wisps, screwed up to receive skimpy ounces and quarters, but capacious bags, that would stand squarely on end when filled and corded, and that you would not err in describing as one pound of two-and-tuppenny tea, and four of tuppenny-ha'penny soft sugar.

This was, of course, magnificent; still one might have thought that old Mrs. Kilfoyle's recollections of earlier days, remote though they were, would have prevented her from being so taken aback as to sit with the packages in her lap remarking nothing more appropriate than, "Musha then—well to goodness—sure woman dear—och now begorrah—why, what at all"—treble-noted incoherencies, which were borne down by the gruffer tones of Mrs. M'Gurk, who at the same time was saying, over-earnestly for a mere conventional disclaimer: "Ah now, Mrs. Kilfoyle, honey, don't let there be a word out of your head. Sure it was just to gratify meself I done it, for I'm rael annoyed—divil a lie I'm tellin' you—it's downright annoyed I do be to see the little tay-pot sittin' cocked up there on the shelf, and niver a dhrop to go in it for you this great while back."

"Ay, that's so," said Mrs Brian, "nary a grain o' tay she's had sin' poor Thady went, that would be bringin' her an odd quarter-poun' when he was after gettin' a job of work anywheres. But these times, what wid this thing and the other—How-ane'er it's a grand tays she'll be takin' now entirely," continued Mrs. Brian, who was inwardly calling herself a big stupid gomach for alluding to Thady, "and the goat's milkin' finely yet awhile, so as there'll be a sup o' milk for her. You'll be havin' great tay drinkins now, mother, won't you, wid what all Mrs. M'Gurk's after bringin' you?"

But: "The paice of heaven be his sowl's rest," Mrs. Kilfoyle said, as if to herself, with an irrelevancy which showed that her daughter-in-law had failed to turn back the current of her thoughts.

"I'm sure it was oncommon friendly of you, ma'am," Mrs. Brian said to Mrs. M'Gurk, with a semi-reproachful emphasis, which was addressed to some one else.

"'Deed, and that it was," the little old woman responded, remembering her manners, which she very seldom forgot, and hastening back from—who knows where? "There's nothin' I fancy like me cup o' tay; and you to be thinkin' of that. Why, I'll get Norah here to wet us a drop this mortial instiant."

"But Mrs. M'Gurk—why musha Mrs. M'Gurk," an exciting possibility had just occurred to one of the neighbours who were seeing her home—"what's gone wid your bag of male all this while? Where have you it at all? Glory be to goodness, woman alive, it's not after lavin' it behind you anywheres you are?"

"Set it down out of her hand belike—or Stacey it was maybe—and it's twenty-siven chances if iver she sees sight or light of it agin."

"Well, well, well, begorrah, to think of that happenin' the crathur."

"Male is it?" said the widow, with calm. "Sure was it breakin' me own back or the girl's I'd be carryin' a load o' male that far? I could git one of the lads to bring me up a stone handy the next time he's down beyant—That's to say, if I'd make me mind up to be spendin' money on it at all,' Mrs. M'Gurk hastened to add, being well aware that thruppince farthin' was at present the amount of her capital; "I've no great opinion of male meself. It's a brash. A good hot pitaty's a dale tastier any day."

When Mrs. M'Gurk finally completed her unpacking in the seclusion of her own cabin, it appeared that she had brought nothing home with her except a penn'orth of salt. The small brown-paper bag did not present an imposing appearance, set solitary on the bare deal table, and she stood looking at it with a somewhat regretful expression for a few moments. She was saying to herself: " If they'd axed an anyways raisonable price for them red woolly wads"—she meant knitted comforters— "hangin' up at Corr's, I might ha' got one for Mrs. Sheridan's Joe. It's starved wid the could the imp of a crathur does be, and she's hard set to keep a stitch to its back. But sivenpence-ha'penny's beyond me altogether."

However, perfect satisfaction is unattainable, and few women have felt more contented, on the whole, with the result of a day's shopping than did Mrs. M'Gurk as she tumbled into the rushes and rags of her curiously constructed lair, where she began to dream of tobacco, and yarn, and alluring bakers' windows in the middle of her first strangely worded *Hail Mary.*

CHAPTER III.

ONE TOO MANY.

IT may have been partly the widow M'Gurk's American windfall that turned people's thoughts thitherward, by making them realise vividly the advantages of receiving remittances from abroad ; at any rate it is certain that throughout the following winter the idea of emigration to " the States " was unwontedly in the air at Lisconnel. Not that it throve or spread there to any considerable extent, this cabin-cluster being one of those forlorn, makeshift, casual-looking little settlements wherein the inhabitant seems always to strike a terribly deep and tenacious root. Primarily, it may be, from a self-preserving instinct, for his shaggy roof and stony scrap of potato-plot form his stronghold, his first and last outpost against the ever-beleaguering wilderness and solitary places, and he clings to them with a desperation hardly conceivable by people who interpose more elaborate barriers between their lives and the sheer brute forces of nature. Outside that screed of rough shelter he knows what ills forthwith await him, what stepmotherliness of barren earth, what pitilessness of capricious skies, but there is nothing in his experience to apprise him of any counterbalancing good. All his auguries drawn from thence are of privation : solitude, silence—or uncomforting strange faces and voices—homelessness, hunger—these things promise to be his portion when once he passes beyond the reach of his fragrant blue turf smoke and his big black pot. And from such-like evils " th' ould place at home " has hitherto shielded him more or less effectually ; but furthermore it provides him with a daily ration of business and desire, a clue to guide his wanderings through the mazes of a destiny that at best seems to him sufficiently perplexing and inscrutable. For he has, as a rule, too much imagination, and too little of more material things, to keep his mind clear of fateful riddles. Therefore he puts habit and familiarity in the stead of understanding, and thinks he sees " some sinse and raison " in his own townland and neighbours, because he has all his life been used to the look of them, and to their ways. But the very aspect of a strange place makes him feel as lost and helpless as a leaf blown from its bough ; and herein his plight has some resemblance—thus do extremes meet—to that of the great German philosopher, whose working powers were gravely imperilled by the threatened felling of a tree, which had stood in sight of his study window.

His " bit o' land," then, is dear to the dweller in Lisconnel, not mainly *as* a bit of land, but rather as the fragment of solid tangible fact, contact with which keeps his whole existence from becoming the sport of meaningless mysteries, in somewhat the same fashion that we have seen one of his superfluous boulders keep the wind from whirling his thatch dispersedly about the bog. Nor is this a stone picked up and flung on at random. It is bound down securely with strong ties of memories and associations, twined through long years, and to be broken by no storm-gusts of circumstance. A meagre field-fleck and a ramshackle shanty on the hill's wan gray slope, or the lip of the black-oozing morass, is scarcely an ideal earthly paradise ; yet it may be at least the site of the only one that can appear possible for him. There are invisible fixtures in his cavernous-interiored cabin, which a law, not included probably in the code enforced by landlords and sub-sheriffs, forbids him to remove. This inconvenient non-transferability of affections would prove an obstacle in the way of compensation for disturbance, or any similar grievance which a relenting fate might seek to redress. Should a sequence of calamity such as

Job's overtake him, sweeping away his flocks and herds and children, no eventual doubling of his live stock could console him, as it did the more philosophic sheikh. His last days would still be made darker than his first by many a regret for "the ould white heifer," or "the little red cow," or "the bit of a skewbald pony, the crathur." And as for the ten new sons and daughters — Molly and Biddy and Katty—they would be a failure indeed.

Persons with this turn of mind are obviously not likely to favour any emigration project, and, as I have said, the idea never became popular in Lisconnel, where, to be sure, its merits were seldom considered at all dispassionately. To the older people emigration simply seemed much the same thing as death, with the aggravating circumstance that it chiefly menaced the childer and the boys; they discussed it in the same tone that they would have adopted in talking about the outbreak of some dangerous epidemic. Even the young men and lads, who did now and then glance at the possibility —to summarily dismiss it—kept their meditations, for the most part, to themselves. It was too tragical a subject to be utilised upon trivial occasions of discontent or ruffled vanity, as their brethren sometimes recall disaffected mothers and sisters to their allegiance, by dark hints dropped about the feasibility of enlisting.

In only one household at Lisconnel was the idea entertained at this time with any degree of approbation, and even there from what may be called a vicarious point of view. I refer to the Sheridans, who live in the cabin nearest the Kilfoyles and Mick Ryans. They were in those days a large straggling family, ranging from Andy, who was one-and-twenty, and stood six-foot-three in his stockings—when he wore any—to a half-brother, who had but lately begun to crawl away when set down on the ground, which newly-acquired habit disarranged the calculations of any person responsible for the whereabouts of his tattered red flannel frock. For Peter Sheridan had married twice, and his first wife's family of four were now supplemented by a flock of seven or eight. Second marriages are not well thought of in Lisconnel, and Peter, a gloomy-tempered man, who had few social gifts, did not raise himself in the public esteem by taking up with Mattie Duggan. The neighbours were of the opinion that "poor Molly Mahony's childer would be apt to find the differ"; but Mattie did not turn out a typical stepmother. In fact she was rather good to her youngest stepdaughter, Peg, who was lame, and she was decidedly proud of the well-grown Andy, while she never displayed an unfriendly spirit towards the other two, Sally and Larry. If she helped in getting up the domestic agitation of which I am going to speak, she took no more active part in it than did Larry's own kith and kin. And it may be said for all of them that circumstances were urgent and coercive.

It was a hard winter for everybody, but especially for the Sheridans, who have the name of being an unlucky family. This time their potatoes were much worse than most other people's; it was quite impossible to imagine that their stock could hold out till July, and as they had also lost a fat pig, and had a clutch of eggs addled in an August thunderstorm, it seemed hard to say how they should come by yellow meal wherewith to fill up the hiatus. Himself, that is Peter, the head of the household, had during the last two or three years been growing more and more crippled with rheumatism, and was now quite past his work, which diminished the amount of harvest earnings, and increased an embarrassing deficit on rent-days. So that altogether the state of affairs was one that makes "long" families feel keenly how numerous they are at meal-times, and from this sense there is a natural transition to reflections upon the desirability of larger supplies or a smaller party. The evident impracticability of the former alternative was what at the outset led the Sheridans to take the latter into consideration, very vaguely, indeed, and with no definite purpose. But as they dwelt upon it, the notion gradually developed an outline.

Stray reports came up from the Town about a fortnightly steamer which had lately begun to ply between Kenport and Queenstown, the starting-point of that awful voyage over "oceans of say." Now, Kenport lies within a few days' tramp, not so hopelessly remote but that it was just possible to imagine a man's making his way thither, and once arrived there, persons, so rumour ran, were to be found who would hold themselves responsible for his disembarkation somewhere on the other side, an arrangement which seemed to render further imaginings unnecessary. And when the Sheridans mentally pictured some one they knew trudging off along the familiar road, till it grew strange, and at last going on board the steamboat, stranger still, the figure they saw was Larry, the second boy. Everything pointed him out as the appropriate emigrant. His younger brothers were not old enough, and Andy was out of the question, growing yearly more important in his family circle as his father's infirmities increased. "Sure, we'd be lost' intirely without Andy." Larry, on the contrary, appeared in no wise indispensable. He was twenty years old, almost as tall as his brother, and still growing, but lank and weedy, never to be nearly so fine a figure of a man. Neither had he Andy's practical abilities and energy, being in truth scatter-brained and innately lazy. He loved to sit dangling his long legs on the top of a dyke, or to lie basking on a sun-warmed bank ; and, especially in winter time, when the uncomfortable outer world became a fact to ignore as much as possible, he was very fond of getting into a few tattered sheets of an old song-book and a loose-leaved volume of *Ivanhoe*, picked up goodness knows where, and presented to him by the widow M'Gurk, who had also taught him his letters. It is true that his long legs would run miles ungrudgingly on an errand if anybody was took bad, or in trouble, and that his most foolish actions were often done with the kindest intentions. It was true, too, that ever and anon upon some emergency he would make some shrewd suggestion, which caused his neighbours to remark that Larry Sheridan was no fool when he chose to leave wool-gathering and give his mind to what he was about. Whereupon some person present would probably add that he was a dacint poor lad any way, and a rael gob o' good-nature. But all this did not alter the stubborn fact that his services were not, and could not be, worth his keep, since at the busiest times the Sheridans' tiny holding scarcely gave full employment to Andy and Tim, not to mention Sally and the smaller fry ;

while at slack seasons Hercules himself could merely have kicked his heels there rather more vigorously than ordinary mortals.

In short, when once his relations had familiarised themselves with the idea, the main obstacle to Larry's departure from Lisconnel lay in his own sentiments on the subject. It would be difficult to overstate their strength. His shrinking from new paths and devotion to old ones exaggerated, well-nigh caricatured, those propensities as commonly exhibited by his neighbours. I do not believe that with his own good will he would ever have gone out of sight of the little knockawn with its lowly crest of grey-gleaming crag. Business now and then called him down to Duffclane, or even as far as the Town; but on these occasions reluctant went his departing steps, and his rising spirits always jumped up several degrees in one bound at the moment when his thatch with its dark-rimmed smoke-hole came into view again from the brow of the hill. To live on where and as he had lived ever since his memories began, was a prospect in which, had it been assured to him, he would have more than acquiesced. Changes of every kind were hateful to him; those wrought slowly by mere lapse of time, even now, at twenty years old, filled him with despondency whenever he thought of them; but he had a faculty for holding aloof from painful reflections, unless they were thrust unavoidably upon his attention.

Of course, with the rest of Lisconnel, he had his share of bad seasons, when sheer want, like a freshet in an ever-brimming stream, comes down upon the household by its brink, and swamps everybody impartially. From his normal circumstances, however, that is when he had not overmuch to do, and pretty nearly enough to eat, he drew whole daysful of content, lounging away his leisure amid a happy mingling of accustomed sights and sounds with fantastic dreams partly inspired by the confused glimpses of mediæval romance, which he spelled out for himself. These glimpses were made all the more confused by the necessity he was under of sorting as best he could the pages of his dishevelled volume, which, carefully though he stowed them away, got mixed up, as a rule, between each reading, and probably were never replaced just in the order Sir Walter had intended. Once Larry had given little Pat his brother "a clout on the head" for mischievously jumbling them all together again, and this act of violence was one of his life's two most remorseful memories. The other was the recollection of how, at about five years old, he had one day furtively finished a potato, which his mother, who died soon afterwards, had been eating for her dinner, when a neighbour called her to the door with some message, and how he had seen her look disappointed on her return as she missed the remnant of her stinted meal. Both these incidents were apt to haunt him during his rare absences from home, and by some curious train of thought they made him feel somehow that it would be a judgment on him if "anythin' went agin the others" while he was away. Whence we may infer that if Larry Sheridan's count of crimes were a heavy one, his conscience must have been gravely deficient in the faculty of selection.

It was a long time ere Larry began to have the faintest inkling of the plans which his family were forming on his behalf. His habit of mind was somewhat inobservant, and the enormity of the idea, as it appeared to him, made him the slower to take it up. But when it did dawn upon him, he was nearly as much shocked as he would have been had he detected the rest in a conspiracy for drowning him in the bog-hole at the back of their house. Thenceforward he became feverishly alive to every word or look that could conceivably bear on the matter. For it must not be supposed that Larry's people told him explicitly how expedient they considered his departure to the States. Such plainness of speech is not our custom in Lisconnel, where we are on the one hand innately averse from stating in cold blood facts likely to displease our hearers, and, on the other, are quickwitted enough to take hints with a readiness which allows things of the kind to be conveyed under a muffle of innuendo, thus avoiding some disagreeable friction at the cost of a little candour, and an occasional risk of misapprehension. To my mind the bargain is, on the whole, not a bad one for us, who want all the amenities of life that come by any means within our reach. If Larry had charged anybody point-blank with wishing him to emigrate, he would have elicited a vehement disclaimer. " Och now, the saints in glory be among us—the goodness grant me patience wid him—is it ravin' the lad is? Sure what talk has e'er a one of any such a thing? We were just passin' the remark that out there appears to be a fine place, where a young chap 'll git his livin' aisy and to spare, instead of scrapin' an ould pot where there's maybe plenty widout him to be scrapin' it. Howane'er it's long sorry I'd be to bid anybody go make his fortin against his will." But his mind, fairly sensitised, received to his sorrow, the import of insinuations far more delicately wrapped up than this hypothetical one. Sometimes he caused himself needless pangs by imagining hints where none were meant ; he never escaped any through lack of perception.

Of course he did not "let on." To have overtly

recognised the existence of the project would have seemed to bring it a stage nearer execution. But though he said nothing, he took action upon it. For he reasoned with himself that he must have been a great little-good-for, and a blamed ould handless bosthoon, or else the rest of them would never have took up with a notion of getting shut of him. And the conclusion which he deduced was to the effect that if he showed himself in a more favourable light, they might be led to dismiss the idea. He remembered now regretfully how often he had lain *perdu* behind his favourite big boulder, while his step-mother was audible in the distance screeching for some one to fetch her a "bucket o' wather," and he resolved to turn over a new leaf. Indeed he seemed, so to speak, to turn over several at once, for he fell to bringing in so many bucketfuls that his sister Sally asked him with sarcasm whether he thought they were about making themselves *a young lough* in the middle of the flure. It was not easy to find channels for all his new industrial zeal. Once he nearly broke his back by hauling a heavy, snaggy black mass, half root, half tree-trunk, up to their door from a distant turf-cutting, because he had heard Mrs. Sheridan say that it would make a grand stool like, for beside the hearth corner. But having left it thus overnight, with the intention of just "rowlin' it in handy" the first thing next morning, behold the earlier Andy accomplished this while Larry still slept, and entered lightly into all the *kudos* of the toilsome achievement.

The children naturally quarrelled all day for the glory of occupying the new seat, and in the course of their contention Paddy tumbled little Rosanne head-foremost into the hearth, and was within "an ame's ace of settin' the innicent child in a blaze of fire." Whereupon their mother remarked that she "wished to goodness that big gomeral Larry would let alone litterin' up the place wid his ould sticks, and encouragin' the childer to destroy themselves. Sure if he could find nothin' better to be after at home, there were places where there was plenty besides mischief to be doin'." To which Sally rejoined, "Ay, bejabers, are there," with a flash of the recurrent thought that, if young Dan O'Beirne knew she had a brother doin' well in the States, and sendin' home poun's and poun's, he might not think such a wonderful heap of Stacey Doyne, a girl whose people were as poor as they could stick together. So inapparent may be the links between cause and effect.

Many another little scheme of Larry's proved equally unsuccessful, yet he did not relax his efforts. Some of his attempts to propitiate seem rather melancholy. He was more careful than ever to avoid making his presence felt obtrusively around the steaming pot, sometimes keeping away altogether, and sometimes saying imaginatively: "Bedad, Tim, you must halve this wi' me, anyways; she's after givin' me enough to feed a rigiment of horse and fut." He even exerted himself to secure the suffrages of the small children, who were already well affected towards him, by unusual alacrity in acceding to their requests for performances of a farcical song and dance, known in the family as "Larry's antics." His grotesque capers often were cut to a tragic accompaniment of very unmirthful meditations—such Œdipean choruses will attend our comic operas; however, this took nothing from the pleasure of his unsuspecting audience. It appeared a graver drawback that the entertainment was liable to be prohibited summarily by a growl from Peter, who through those slow-gaited winter days formed a centre of domestic gloom where he sat beside the fire, fearing that he would never be good for a stroke of work again, and ever and anon diversifying his discomfortable private cogitations by a captious excursion into the affairs going forward around him. On evenings when his mood was more disconsolate than usual, the first flourish of Larry's arms and legs would produce a peremptory injunction to "quit carryin' on like a deminted

ONE TOO MANY. 55

scare-crow in a storm o' win';" and Larry would have to desist from that artful method of ingratiation.

About this time, if any explorers of Lisconnel had come across a long, ragged youth seated on a grey-lichened boulder, ruffling up a halo of black hair with both hands, and staring before him over the bog with a whole horizonful of melancholy in his wide, dark eyes and narrow, peaked face, they would probably have seen Larry Sheridan engaged in earnestly pondering and planning how he could induce his family to let him live out his bit of life among them, unmolested by nightmare visions of being driven off into the great, strange, miserable world—away from Lisconnel.

In all these aims and devices, Larry enjoyed the encouragement and comfort of one sympathising coadjutrix—his sister Peg. A close friendship had existed between them from her earliest days, when Larry used to carry her about to a surprising extent, considering that he was the elder by only three years. And as she grew older without ever learning to walk rightly, it was Larry who did most to make her amends for this privation. He spent hours in amusing her; and at one time even wished to teach her to read, that she might be able to entertain herself with his priceless library. But Peg, who was practical-minded, showed no enthusiasm for literature. In fact, when he tried to begin her second lesson, she immediately kicked him, saying, with a howl, "Git along wid your ugly ould *Ah, Bay, Say*," and tore one of his precious pages nearly in half, thereby abruptly finishing her education.

However, despite their dissimilarity of taste and her occasional shortness of temper, their friendship continued to thrive, and Peg now manifested it by vigorously siding with Larry in the queer undeclared struggle which was going on beneath their roof. It is true that Peg was no very powerful auxiliary; still she had zeal, and some intelligence, which enabled her to act not inefficiently as trumpeter of all Larry's worthy deeds, and forager for facts wherewith to rebut those advanced in support of their views by the opposite party. Thus, if Larry cleared a path through the snow-drift, or brought home the hen that had foosthered off with herself down the bog, or mended the worst hole in the thatch, beneath which the drip had begun to form a *deep* pool, Peg made it her business to see that all influential members of the household were duly apprised of these services. But she drew a discreet veil over the less quotable incidents of his first attempt at roof-patching on a plan of his own, namely, the insertion into the aperture of an old meal-bag stuffed with stones, and her hairbreadth escape of being brained by a shower of them, which the speedy collapse of the rotten sacking let tumble into the room. Or, again, her step-mother might observe regretfully, as she threw the uneatably bad potatoes into a heap for the benefit of the widow M'Gurk's pig: "Sure, it's a poor case to be makin' waste for the feedin' of other people's fat bastes. Judy Ryan was sayin' she'd heard tell the Dunnes' son below, that's away off somewheres abroad this two year, was after sendin' them home the price of a grand young pig, they'll be gettin' oodles o' money on at the fair afore Lent. But ah, sure, where's there anybody to do us a hand's turn? as I sez to her." But there Peg would be, ready primed to countermine this anecdote with Mrs. Quigley's cousin, who had never had a day's health ever since he had gone off to live away at Shanasheen, and a man Brian Kilfoyle knew, who went up to the north ten year ago, and had never been heard of from that good day to this. Brian thought like enough somethin' might ha' happint him.

Considered as arguments, Peg's little narratives may not appear particularly cogent; yet much further-fetched ones were resorted to by both factions. Even Mad Bell's and Crazy Christie's contributions on the question were not disregarded. Indeed, Mrs. Sheridan laid no small stress upon

Bell's report of a conversation which, during one of her rambles, she had had with a man lately returned from New York. It varied in details from time to time, but was substantially to the effect that, " In thim parts, if there's anythin' ye're a-wantin', all ye've got to do is to turn a handle round and round a few odd times, and there you are, wid no more trouble about it." " So maybe," Mrs. Sheridan would comment, finding herself unable to accept this scheme of things in quite all its beautiful simplicity, " the crathur hasn't exactually comperhinded the rights of it ; but if there's any sense in it at all at all, that must be an uncommon convanient country to git one's livin' in."

The experiences of the O'Driscoll family were of course made to do yeoman's service on Larry's side ; but that is a mournful history which must have a chapter to itself.

So this winter dragged on heavily towards lengthening days, and Larry at times thought hopefully that when the open spring weather came, and the potato-setting and turf-cutting began, he would be the better able to demonstrate his *raison d'être* at Lisconnel ; while in moments of despondency he felt as if his will were being sapped by the continued assaults of public opinion, till he must needs surrender himself to the conviction that it was his duty to go away and burden his family no longer. But it was well on towards the end of March, when there occurred what seemed to him a grand opportunity of proving himself capable and useful—a member of the establishment whom " the rest of them " would think twice of wishing to transport.

One forenoon, Biddy and Paddy and Johnny and Katty and Rosanne and Joe—the last-named waddled a long way behind the others, and could not as yet roar articulately—came bawling home with the news that Andy was just after taking the hand off of him with his ould clasp-knife down below fornint Hughey Quigley's turf-stack. This was happily an exaggerated version of the disaster; but Andy really had given his right wrist an ugly gash, which obliged him to seek surgical aid from Dan O'Beirne, the blacksmith at Duffclane, and which threatened to cripple him for some little time to come. It was a vexatious accident, for the slowly-relaxing frosts had at last allowed people to think of getting in their potatoes, already belated enough. Lisconnel always breathes more freely when once its potatoes are down, and the earlier the better, for every reason. The likelihood of a good crop is increased, and people have a soothing sub-consciousness that something is all the while being done on their behalf out of sight among the trenches and lazy-beds. Their stock of seed, too, is thus ensured against the possibility of being desperately eaten in any crisis of short commons. So much, however, depended on the crop, that the Sheridans thought it prudent to await Andy's convalescence, rather than proceed with their sowing while he was incapacitated; and works therefore came to a standstill in the plot behind their cabin.

It chanced one morning a few days later that Larry, returning from an early ramble, found most of his family absent. Andy, accompanied by several of his brethren, had gone to O'Beirne the blacksmith, and the others were somewhere out on the bog, leaving only the stiff-jointed Peter and limping Peg at home. Peter was never cheerful company, and Peg to-day would do nothing but cower over the fire with her knitting, for she was suffering from a bad fit of neuralgia, or, as she put it, was "destroyed entirely wid the face-ache." Larry accordingly went out of doors again in quest of entertainment. It was a grim, rayless morning, the horizon veiled round and round with a dusky, powdery haze, of the peculiar hue and texture seen only on a day possessed by the devil of an east wind. That wind, too, showed all its distinctively vicious qualities in an exalted degree. Its piercing fangs seemed to have been whetted on a myriad icebergs, and its bitter blasts to breathe from over continents of shrouding snow; it was a wind that simultaneously stung and benumbed, that felt dankly chill as the touch of a drowned hand, and yet parched aridly as if its mission were to bake the veins of the earth with frost. The very grass-blades it passed over seemed to lose colour and to shiver stiffly, as if their sap were congealed. But Larry did not trouble himself about the cold, for he had scarcely crossed the swampy patch that brought him to their little field when he was seized by a great idea. There lay the half-dug trenches, which had been begun on the day before Andy's accident, with tools strewn around ready to hand whenever work should be resumed, and Larry suddenly resolved that *he* would undertake it now. It would be a grand thing, he said to himself, if he could get down, at any rate, a good few of those potatoes over which his father was at the present minute helplessly fuming and fretting in his gloomy corner He would set about it at once, before anybody knew what he was doing. No one had ever suggested his attempting such a thing, because indeed no one would have dreamed of entrusting so critical a task to a quare blundering gaby like Larry; therefore he had not any prohibitions or scoffs to give him pause, and he felt strongly that the accomplishment of the feat single-handed would prove a splendid feather in his cap.

Thus inspired he fell to forthwith, and toiled hugely, until when he broke off, and leaned panting on his spade to review his labours, a considerable portion of the narrow plot lay ready for the seed. To give him his due, the spade-work, which he contemplated with all your jack-a-dream's peculiar pride and satisfaction in any casual bit of practical achievement, had been thoroughly and properly done, and so far things were well enough. But Larry had determined to make a job of it, and not to desist until his drills were safely planted. So he fetched a bag of the seed potatoes from their nook behind the turf-heap indoors, unbeknownst to his father and Peg. "Musha," he said with guile, to account for his rustling, "I'm just drivin' th'ould hen off of roostin' on Sally's ould shawl"—and he presently was seated on the low wall, scientifically slicing away with the worn stump of knife-blade, two inches long, which had cut out the Sheridan family's "eyes" for many a season's crop. The last pale whitey-brown section had been earthed over, and Larry was dealing a few superfluous final pats with the flat of his broad *griffawn*, congratulating himself the while that he had got through undisturbed, and could now display his doings as a triumphant surprise, when

Peg came halting out of doors and up to the field-dyke. Her eye was at once caught by the dangling potato-sack, and in a moment she had surmised the whole calamity.

"Mercy on us all alive, Larry," she said, "you've niver been meddlin' with the pitaties this day?"

"Bedad have I," quoth Larry, with a cheerfulness half bravado, for Peg's tone awakened a horrible foreboding, which he dared not face; "look at the rows I've got set, and good luck to them. Sure it's great weather I've made of it this mornin' entirely."

"Then it's lost we are. The blight's in the win', and sorra the thrace of a one of them 'll iver be seen above the ground."

Larry all at once knew that it was very cold. His own hands were benumbed, and an icy grasp suddenly clutched at his heart. Peg had spoken truly: the east wind had brought with it, like a lurking assassin, the murderous black frost, which stabs and slays all life and growth in its frail first beginnings. And in the teeth of that he had cut up and planted nearly a bagful of their hoarded seed potatoes. He stared blankly round the hard hodden-grey sky, and then at the neighbours' little brown fields, where never a soul was working, and then at the rush-fringed puddle on Peg's side of the dyke, and he saw that its edges had gathered a flaky ice-film. "Thrue—thrue for you," he faltered, and stood looking helplessly from the flaccid sack to the smooth-swelling ridges, a haggard and tatterdemalion Despair.

"Ye great stupid mischief-makin' gomeral," said Peg, "ye meddlin' good-for-nothin' jackass, that can't keep your hands off interferin' wid what ye've no call to be touchin'. Look at what you're afther doin' on us—the best part of a sackful as good as slung down a bog-houle. Sure little Paddy'd ha' known better than to be cuttin' and sowin' on the one day, let alone when the air's teemin' wid the black frost. Och, but it's a heart-scald to have the likes of such a sthookawn stravadin' about lookin' out for harrum to be doin' and throuble to make. It's no more than the truth they're spakin' when they do be sayin' ye'd a right to take off yerself out o' this to some place where ye might ruinate and desthroy all before you, and no matter to us. That's all ye're fit for, so it is. Just wait till father and Andy hare tell of it—just wait, ye big omadhawn, standin' there star-gazin' like a stuck pig. The tomfoolery of you would annoy an ould crow. Och, wirra such a thing to go do; I'm fairly sickened wid you, and that's a fac'. Of all the bosthoons——"

Peg expressed herself as forcibly as we should have done if confronted at equally close quarters with a prospect of more than semi-starvation. She was further exasperated by a sense that her ally had irretrievably disgraced and discredited her partisanship. Altogether her feelings were so much perturbed that she did not remark how silent Larry was, neither attempting any defence nor, as would have been more characteristic, breaking out into vehement self-abuse. He only said, as he gazed down the length of a freshly drawn furrow, "And all the while I might as well have been diggin' me grave."

On the following morning Larry was not indoors at breakfast-time, which did not surprise his angered family, as he often roamed off early, and on this occasion had no reason to anticipate an enjoyable meal. But Peg was soon afterwards rather astonished at finding his two "ould flitthers of books" stuffed into the niche in the wall where she kept her knitting and yarn, for he always stowed them away carefully in a receptacle of their own. And about sunset Andy, returning from the blacksmith's, brought the news how Larry had passed by there in the grey of the morning, going towards the Town, and had left word with Dan O'Beirne that he was off to Kenport, where he would get a passage in the American steamer. Then Peg knew that Larry's library was a farewell gift. Everybody else thought that the whole thing was just a bit of blathers like, and that they would have him streeling home again in a couple of days; but Peg from the first said, " Niver a fut."

The weeks which converted all the others to her opinion passed heavily for her. Desertion of your comrade at a pinch is an ill-favoured spectre to look back upon under any circumstances, and when the chances seem to be all against your ever more having an opportunity of making amends for your defection, it often grows so fascinatingly hideous that you cannot easily look the other way. Peg in those days met it at every turn, looming lividly against a cloud of reminiscence, which was rapidly becoming charged with remorse. Nor under its oppressive lowering could she find any clearer gleam of consolation than the chance that Larry might some day be writing home, perhaps from the unknown regions of Queenstown, or at any rate from wherever he came to in the States. And then, Peg thought to herself, she would get Brian Kilfoyle to scrawm a letter for her—she had pennies enough to buy the stamp—and bid him to come back to them out of that by the next boat, and never to be minding about the old pitaties; they didn't matter a thraneen. Or maybe by some manner of means she could even send him through the post the pair of socks she had just finished knitting to sell at Corr's. She felt that if she could do that, the throbbing pang might go out of her life, and leave only an endurable ache. But it grew worse and worse while she waited for Larry's letter.

She told her family how lovely it was up on the ridge since the weather had grown so soft, disingenuously leading them to infer that she sat there all day to enjoy the beauties of nature, whereas in truth the gentle April breezes and mild daisy and forget-me-not sky merely enabled her to concentrate her whole attention undiverted upon her watch along the ribbon of road. Another thing they did was to bring on very fast the potatoes, now all planted. Even Larry's unchancy rows had not missed after all, for they showed little green shoots, at the sight of which his half-sister Biddy, a good-natured child, nearly cried her eyes out. But Peg could do nothing better than call herself a black-hearted baste, which was cold comfort, and say passionately to little Johnny, who shouted to her, jubilant at the discovery, " Och whisht, and bad manners to you, you moidherin' brat ; you're all the one thing !"—which was no comfort worth speaking of at all. However, by this time the tidings she waited for so impatiently were already on their road.

People who do not dwell too many leagues beyond man's life, can count upon the advantage, if advantage it be, of receiving their bad news in a flash within an hour or so after date, although their hopes may have gone to wrack on the hot sands under an eastern sunblaze, while they were groping businesswards through a London fog. But such things come to Lisconnel by much more circuitous routes. During those April days Peg's messenger, by slow stages of stone-dyked countryside, between ever smaller and lonelier hamlets, was making his way thither in the person of a little feeble-gaited *sprissawn* of a man, who looked as if he had escaped from a vampire-cave, but who in reality had been lately discharged from the workhouse infirmary at Kenport.

He appeared in Lisconnel one amber-wested evening, under the delusion that he had arrived at Sallinbeg, for he had strayed many miles out of his weary way; and he was so tired and "took-a-back," that he had not spirits to launch into speech at any length until after the supper to which Hughey Quigley made him welcome, and which Mrs. Pat Ryan enriched with the "sup of thick milk" she had saved for the morning's breakfast.

Then in the course of the conversation, which had drawn several of the neighbours to Quigley's, the stranger remarked in his plaintive southern sing-song: "Now that I remimber, there was a chap from these parts I met wid, and I laid up down away there—Lisconnel, ay bedad, it was there he said he come from; but the name of him's out of me head this instiant—a young slip of a lad wid legs to him the length of a three-month foal's. Och begorrah, I've got him after all—Sheridan— that's what it was sure enough—Larry Sheridan."

Peg was the only one of her family who happened to be present, crouched unobtrusively round an angle of the dresser. If she had been a wild creature in a forest, you would now have thought she had heard a twig snap.

"'Deed then, that will ha' been Peter Sheridan's Larry – him that's took off to the States. Well now, to think of your fallin' in wid him."

" The States?—sure enough he had great talk of the States out of him; but be the time he come into the infirm'ry he wasn't fit to be thravellin' the len'th of the ward, that indifferent he was, let alone skytin' over the ocean-says."

" To the infirm'ry, was you sayin'? Sakes alive sure what at all ailed the misfortnit bein'? Goodness pity him, to be took bad, and he in a strange place. But niver a hap'orth had the crathur amiss wid him when he quit out of this."

"'Twas an awful could he'd got on the chest; I'm tould they put a grand title to it in the paper. Faith, I took as sarious a one meself, ivery inch of it, but the doctor said he was perished and starved wid thrampin' about in the sevare weather. Howsome'er, his mind was dead set on the emigration. He lay next bed to mine, and I would be harin' him axin' continyal if the Queenstown boat did be about startin' yet. So the Sisters knew well enough he was disthressin' himself for fear she'd be off widout him, and just to pacify him they'd declare be this and be that she was lyin' there alongside the quay, wid ne'er a thought o' stirrin' in her head —and she, mind you, half-ways to wheriver she might be goin' all the while.

"Och now the Sisters do be rael charitable ladies: there was one of them used to bring me the half of her own bit of dinner of a day I didn't fancy what I had for meself. Well, one evenin' he took a bad turn, a sort of wakeness like, and they thought it might be goin' he was, and they sent afther the doctor in a hurry. But be that time he was somethin' better agin, and the doctor seemed a thrifle put out at bein' called onnecessary. 'It's another false alarrum ye've given me, Sister Theresa,' sez he. Anyway, when the young fellow began axin' afther the steamboat, the doctor tould him shortish that she was away wid herself three days since, and he might as well be puttin' the notion out of his mind. Sure, when he said that, I heard Sister Theresa goin' *tchuck tchuck* to herself, thinkin' the crathur'd be annoyed, but he seemed all as well contint.

"'Och then, glory be to God,' sez he, 'if th' ould baste's off at last, I can be steppin' home. Bedad but I've been away from them all one while. Maybe they'll not think so bad be this time of them woful ould '—praties I think he said—'and anyway,' sez he, ' Peg 'll make it up wid me for sartin sure.'

"He kep' such talkin' of a Peg he had, that we settled he'd fell out wid his sweetheart about somethin', and run off in a fantigue.

"Then afther that he was aisier than common for a good bit, and niver a word out of him ; but later on in the night, when we were left to mind ourselves, I heard him discoorsin away to himself at a great rate about gittin' up early, and thrampin' home, and comin' over the hill, and I dunno what all besides. So sez I to him—for somewhiles if you'd slip a word in, he'd answer you back raisonable, and otherwhiles he wouldn't take hould of it, but just pluthered along widout harin'—sez I to him : 'That's a fine journey you're regulatin' there,' sez I ; 'div you think you'll iver be able for it to-morra ?'

"' Sure,' sez he, ' I was thinkin' they've took away me ould brogues on me ; but if the Sister's not for givin' me them back agin, I could aisy make a shift to do widout them. For hail, rain, or snow,' sez he, ' I'll be off to-morra.'

"'Ay, be the powers, will you,' sez I, humourin' him in a manner; 'sure it's not an ould pair of brogues, boyo, that'll hinder you of gettin' home.'

"'Troth no,' sez he, 'sure I'd go barefut on me hands and knees to be there agin.'

"'You've a great opinion whativer of that place,' sez I to him"—the stranger glanced towards the door-framed span of faint green twilight sky with an expression which might have signified that though now in a position to form an opinion for himself, he had resolved upon a polite reticence—"and sez he to me: 'Och, man alive, if I could be seein' a sight of it, and the whoule of them agin, sure 'twould just put the life in me, so it would; for all they might ha' been a bit cross wid me the time I was lavin'. Whethen it's meself 'ud be the lucky bosthoon if iver I got the chanst to be sittin' there under the ould bank in the warmth of the sun, along with the bits of books. I'd borry the loan of them now,' sez he, 'from Peg. They're thrash,' she sez, but there was nothin' else I had to be lavin' her. Sure,' sez he, 'I'll git back one way or the other, but it's a long thramp, and there's a quare sort of heaviness in the ould legs of me, and the win' does be could—and it's cruel lonesome. Would you think now,' sez he, peerin' round the head of his bed hopeful like, 'there'd be e'er a chanst you'd come along wid me that far, if your road lies that a-way? 'Twould be great company for me,' he sez.

"'Och murdher,' sez I, 'and is it in any state I am to be thrampin' thramps, and me tore in two wid the awfulest cough at all? No, me fine lad, if you're for quittin' out of this to-morra, 'twill be along wid yourself.' And the young chap seemed rael discouraged at that; fit to cry he looked. Faix, I remimber the face of him, lanin' up there under th' ould night-lamp, wid his hair standin' on ind, and his eyes shinin' out of his head. Howsomediver, he sez presintly, like as if he'd been makin' his mind up to it, 'I must be startin' fine and early,' he sez, 'and that's a fac'—Div ye see iver a glim of light yit comin' at the window?' sez he—and it scarce sthruck twelve o'clock.

"'Sure then, if it's a long thramp you're goin',' sez I, humourin' him in a manner, you perceive, 'you'd betther be takin' a long sleep to strenthen yourself up; and no fear but there's plinty of time afore you'll see daylight.'

"'I will so,' sez he, sleepy like, 'on'y I wish I'd bid good-night to Peg.'

"Well, the next time I woke up, just about day glimmerin', I thought to notice him breathin' a bit quare, and I was considherin' maybe I'd a right to be callin' some one. But thin I knew there'd be throuble if I took to risin' false alarrums; and after a minyit he was quiet enough ; so I just lay still where I was, and nary another stir I heard. But when the Sister come in at six—may the saints have me sowl if the young chap wasn't lyin' there stone-dead—ay, and turnin' could and stiff."

In the general excitement caused by the catastrophe of the strange little man's story, nobody took note of Peg's proceedings or demeanour, and it was not she who brought home the news. Later on, however, her conduct at this crisis of her history became the subject of some unfavourable criticism at Lisconnel.

"I'll give you me word, ma'am," Mrs. Quigley said to a knot of neighbours next day, " I met her this mornin' fornint me house, and when I stopped, passin' by, and was sayin' I was consarned to hear tell of their trouble about poor Larry, and this way and that, she just let a yell at me to whisht talkin', and took off wid her two hands to her ears, like as if I was after reivin' them out of her head, and me merely passin' a friendly remark."

"That Peg's a quare-tempered fairy of a thing," said Mrs. Brian, "and does be mostly as cross as a weasel."

"Well, at all ivints," said Judy Ryan, "it's no credit to her not to have more feelin' in her for that poor lad, and he oncommon good-natured to her when the two of them was but slips of childer together. But it's *too* good-natured Larry always was—Heaven be his bed!"

Even old Mrs. Kilfoyle, who was not prone to censorious judgments, said that it did seem, so to spake, onnatural of her.

But though Peg may not have expressed her feelings conventionally, I believe they were strong and durable, likely, perhaps, to be henceforward as permanent a fact in her life as her lame foot; and that was a long look-out at seventeen. As for her possible consolations, they had been whirled away like blossoms caught in a March gale. She had only one of them left : Larry had been sartin-sure that she would have made it up with him. So she might be worse off after all.

CHAPTER IV.

A WET DAY.

WHEN we meet a stranger or a slight acquaintance on the roads about Lisconnel, we always say it's a fine day, unless it happens to be actually pouring, and then we say it's a fine day *for the country*. I do not know exactly what meaning is attached to the qualifying clause, for the rain may all the time be trampling down the tangled oats and rotting the potatoes—facts which neighbours and friends point out to one another in unambiguous terms. But it appears to be a mode of speech adopted as a seemly cloak for our uppermost thoughts, on somewhat the same principle that we avoid choosing our own engrossing domestic troubles as a topic of conversation in mixed society. Fine days of this peculiar kind often come to Lisconnel in a long, dripping series, and this was the case with one of which I am sometimes reminded when I hear a ballad-singer setting up a hoarse roulade on the other side of the window-sill flower-boxes.

It was towards the end of an extremely wet July, during which the district had been drenched and soaked and steeped as thoroughly as a bundle of flax in a bog-hole, though with no similarly beneficial result; and yet the wet blanket overhead showed as few traces of wear and tear as if it had been spread out for the first time only that morning. From dawn till dusk the sun found not a single thin place to glimmer through like a bad shilling, and the far-distant peaks were not once conjecturable behind the carefully tucked-round curtain of hodden-grey mist. Lisconnel is pretty well case-hardened to damp, as it ought to be, considering its average annual rainfall—never yet gauged. An ordinarily heavy downpour keeps nobody indoors, except when it is accompanied by a high wind. On a wet day a strong gust will send groups of leisurely conversational loiterers flying to their several black thresholds, and set women screeching to their children to come in out of that out of the teems of rain, under which they had been hitherto disporting themselves unmolested. And then Lisconnel puts on a deserted aspect. Still, its inhabitants appear ever and anon at their doorways, much as amphibia rise to the surface to breathe, for the turf-reek, blown back and beaten down, makes an interior atmosphere amidst which the best-seasoned lungs imperatively crave a whiff of fresher air.

This particular morning was wild and blustery, and when Mrs. Kilfoyle and her daughter-in-law stood looking out, nobody was in sight save, tethered on the opposite grass-and-puddle strip, their own black-and-white goat, who had faced away from the wind, and gave one the impression of being lost in thought. That impression was heightened by the manner in which the creature from time to time nodded its head slowly and moodily, as if dissatisfied with the tenor of its meditations. But presently, in a lull between the blasts, a skirl of vocal music rose up suddenly close by—a harsh voice, cracked and quavering, but still strong enough to be produced with startling effect upon the silence.

"Whisht, Norah! is that her agin?" said Mrs. Kilfoyle. "Bedad and it is—*The Colleen Deelish* she's at this time. 'Twill be after puttin' her out they are."

"Very belike," said Mrs. Brian, craning her neck to look as far as she could up the road. "Och, yis; I just got a glimst of the table tiltin' through the door. Now I call that *bruttish*, and it poltho-guin' fit to drownd a water-rat."

"Sure it's little enough she'll trouble herself,

said Mrs. Sheridan, joining the conversation from her adjacent door; "she'd as lief as not be sittin' in the middle of a pool of water, the crathur. But I can see her from here, and she's got grand shelter under the wall of the shed. Bedad, she's cocked up the table on end behind her back, and is croochin' below like an ould hin in a coop. Now, if there was a hap'orth o' wit in her, she might ha' got on one o' her chairs; but maybe the ground's not altogether dhreeped yit, where she is, wid the way the wind's comin'."

"It's a fine thrate of music she's givin' us this mornin', anyhow," said Andy, popping out his head over his step-mother's shoulder. "Yawpy-yowly, hullabaloola, wirramaroory-rory-roory—Och, there was a grand one! I couldn't aquil that now, not if I put stones in me stockin's and howled all night."

Meanwhile, shrill and strident strains continued to proceed from one of the two cabins which stand at a few perches' distance on the Kilfoyles' side of the road—on the left hand, that is, as you come over the knockawn into Lisconnel. It was screened from their view by an intervening turf-stack, or they could have seen outside the door a little pile of furniture stacked leg-in-air, amongst which a white-clad figure crouched in bold relief against the dark ground and wet-blackened wall.

This was Mad Bell, and these were her household gods undergoing temporary ejectment.

I do not know what conjunction of circumstances brought it about, but for many years that cabin, with the low ridge dwindled away behind it and with its door opening on the wide brown bog, was jointly tenanted by Big Anne, Mad Bell, and the Dummy, as queer a trio, maybe, as you could find under one roof in the province of Connaught. Big Anne ranked as responsible head of the establishment, by virtue of characteristics much less markedly divergent from the normal type than those of her co-tenants, both of whom belonged to the category of unaccountable persons, in Lisconnel's opinion "as apt to be doin' one thing as another." She was indeed merely a very tall, large-boned woman, with a habit of walking upon the heels exclusively of enormous feet, which enabled her neighbours to recognise her at great distances by her gait. Nobody would have thought, to look at her, that she was sensitive on the subject of her personal appearance, yet she never did forget or forgive Biddy Sheridan's indiscreet remark that "one fut of Big Anne's would cover two of the flags in the floorin' of the chapel-porch down beyant."

The Dummy, a short squat woman, with a pale broad face and shifty light eyes, was a more exceptional personality, and on the whole rather an unpopular one among us, though Big Anne, who had the best opportunities of judging, always described her as "a *quite* poor crathur," which, under the circumstances, might no doubt be deemed somewhat damnatorily faint praise. To the present day it is a disputed point in Lisconnel whether the Dummy were really dumb or only malingering. There is one fact which tells strongly in favour of those who maintain the thesis "that she could have spoken as plain as any mortial sowl if she'd so pleased," namely, that she assumed total deafness, but evidently was not deaf; for she would start violently if you yelled suddenly into her ear or clattered a heavy stone against the dyke close beside her, experiments which the children never wearied of trying. Hence it is not an unwarrantable conclusion that both infirmities may have been feigned, or at least exaggerated, for professional purposes, the Dummy having in her earlier days led a vagrant life. Upon this hypothesis her persistence in sustaining the character was regarded as unneighbourly. They are obliged, on the other hand, to admit that her success in doing so seemed almost incredibly complete, since no authentic instance has been recorded of her ever having uttered a syllable. Vague rumours are current to the effect that she said something on her death-bed, but few people believe them. It is, however, a well-established fact that the day before she died she laboriously extricated her savings, to the amount of sixpence in silver and twopence in coppers, from a pouch sewn up in her sleeve, and made clear by pantomimic signs how she wished the woman who had befriended her in her last illness to expend the sum on sugarsticks for the children—a testamentary disposition which gave great satisfaction.

As for Mad Bell, her title to insanity rested, perhaps, on a less questionable foundation than the Dummy's pretensions to deafness. It may seem antecedently probable that in an unsophisticated little community like Lisconnel much scope would be found for the development of individuality, and that there, if anywhere, one might strike out unchallenged into unconventional paths. The contrary rather is the case. A very slight deviation from certain recognised lines of conduct suffices there to write you down roundly as mad or crazy, with no euphemistic flourishes of "eccentric" or "peculiar." It is true that the adjectives are used in a considerably less disparaging and disabling sense than they have elsewhere, and that, once fairly appropriated, they confer a license which often permits the holder to do what seems good unto him with more than other men's

A WET DAY. 83

freedom from hampering criticism. Thus, her neighbours said, "Well, Mad Bell, how's yourself this long while?" just as respectfully as if they had addressed her as *missis* or *ma'am*, and nobody thought the worse of her because she now and again "stravaded away wid herself the dear knows where," and might not reappear for weeks or months. I must own that her aspect on this wet day was odd enough. She had lately returned from a protracted excursion, in the course of which somebody had bestowed upon her a huge old white felt Gainsborough hat with blue velvet rosettes and streamers—she must have gone a long, long way from Lisconnel ere she reached the region of such head-gear. This she wore surmounting the folds of a rough white woollen wrap, such as have in these bad times begun to supersede the more expensive blue cloth cloaks of Galway, and her little wedge of yellow face peered out beneath with a goblinish effect. If a wizened lemon could look up shrewdly at you, it would be curiously like Mad Bell's visage. Altogether she was a figure you would have glanced at again, even if you had not come across it sitting among upturned chair and table-legs on the edge of a bog-track, in a downpour of rain, and singing "The Rising of the Moon" at the top of its voice.

Her situation demands an explanatory note.

As a rule, Mad Bell lived on fairly harmonious terms with her house-mates. But she had one idiosyncrasy with which they could not put up. This was an occasional propensity for bursting forth into song, loud, long, and drawn from an apparently inexhaustible *répertoire*, which might have made the fortune of any average street musician. Perhaps Big Anne and the Dummy had unusually sensitive musical ears, or perhaps they had not been educated up to such elaborate performances; for little singing is to be heard in Lisconnel, and that little is seldom more than the low croon to which a woman might put her child asleep or milk her goat. Be this as it may, they could not by any means endure Mad Bell's lays. Accordingly, whenever she "settled herself for a screechin' match"—Big Anne's inappreciative phrase—they adopted summary and stringent measures. Part of the household furniture was understood to be her private property, how acquired nobody clearly knew, though it was commonly associated with the tradition that "Mad Bell had come of very dacint people, mind you. And now the first penetrating notes of one of her interminable ballads were always the signal for her fellow-lodgers to seize upon a couple of rush-bottomed chairs, a small deal table and a little black-looking clothes-horse, all of which they deposited outside the door. I cannot say whether these articles constituted precisely Mad Bell's possessions neither more nor less, or whether the whole act being, so to speak, symbolical and ceremonial, they were merely selected as conveniently portable ; but she never failed to take the graceful hint, and either subsided into silence, or if, as oftener happened, the lyrical impulse proved irresistible, followed her furniture out of doors, and there carolled to her heart's content.

It seemed to have come upon her in great force this morning, for a full hour after her eviction she was still singing lustily, with an impassioned fervour, indeed, which suggested that she must be inspired by some theme admitting of a poignant personal application. Yet the burden of her song was in reality nothing less remote than a string of rather disjointed reflections upon the character of Queen Bess. By that time the wind had sunk away, and the steady patter of drops, which kept the puddles dancing round dances, did not deter the children from standing about to listen. They remained at a wary distance, however, and only those who were furthest off squeaked in mimicry of her most ornate trills and flourishes; for Mad Bell sometimes lost her temper, and was then an alarming person. Judy Ryan once said that to hear her curse was enough to terrify all creation, from the saints sleepin' on their feather-beds o' glory, to the little midge-weevils hatchin' of themselves in the bottoms of the ould bog-holes. But Judy always has had a gift for using impressive figures of speech in moments of agitation. Only the approach of noon, with its prospects of dinner, drew away Mad Bell's audience; and when Lisconnel had finished dining, the concert, too, was over, and she had retreated indoors, chairs, table and all.

At Lisconnel in July, dinner is often something of a failure. You might walk past many of the open doors while it is in progress, without coming upon the pleasant familiar smell of pitaties steaming in their brown jackets. And when that is the case, you may be pretty sure there is no better substitute in the big pot than a "brash" of the gritty yellow Indian-meal, which people must get through as well as they can, thinking themselves lucky if a drop of goat's milk is forthcoming to improve matters for the children. For what with potatoes "going" at the middle, which causes terrible waste, and with one's being prone to fill the pot very full so long as one's heap looks large, not to mention the lending of loans to a neighbour, or the occasional entertainment of some frankly ravenous guest, it seldom or never happens that anybody's store holds out beyond the end of June; while it seldom or never happens, what with late frosts and nipping winds, and cold wet summer weather, that the new crop becomes fit for "lifting" until August is well under way. Hence it follows that July with its soon-glimmering, long-lingering daylight, when one wakens early and has a great many hours to put over before it will be dusk enough to think of sleep again, is even proverbially a month of short-commons and hunger; a Ramadan with no nightly feasting to make up for the day's abstinence; a Lent whose fast no Church ordains and blesses. Its main alleviation has to be sought in the drawing on of harvest-time, which naturally comes uppermost as a topic of conversation. You might have safely laid a wager that at eight out of the nine dinner-parties assembled in Lisconnel on this wet day, prospective potatoes were a theme of discussion, to which a wistful tone was often given by their absence in any more substantial form.

At the Pat Ryans', for instance, Mrs. Pat remarked hopefully, as she distributed little dabs of the thick yellow porridge along the edge of a broken plate to cool for the two youngest children: "Well, I suppose we'll be diggin' next week, please goodness, if the weather's anyways christianable at all."

"And bedad we won't then, after that agin," said her husband, "or maybe the next next week to the back o' that. Sure the forrardest of them's scarce in flower yet, let alone a sign of witherin' on them."

"Some people do say," Mrs. Pat said, looking disconcerted, "that they're fit enough for liftin' the first minyit ye see the colour of a blossom."

"Some people sez more than their prayers," Pat rejoined, with despondent sarcasm, "and fit or no fit, who's to get them dug wid the rain washin' them out o' the ground, you may say, under one's feet? Take care that it's not rotted they'll be on us afore ever they'll have a chanst to ripen. It's much if there isn't a good slam or two of thundher agin we git done wid the wet weather, and that 'ud bring the blight along wid it as ready as anythin'—bad scran to it.... And then there's the turf; sure it had a right to be up dryin' by now, but you might as well go to cut the mud along the roadside. Och, it's a great ould summer we're havin' this time entirely; it's raison to be proud of itself."

Pat dropped his chin dejectedly into his palms as he sat on his black log "forrum," and drew patterns aimlessly on his plastic floor, with the toe of a many creviced brogue. Lisconnel cabin-interiors are all more or less examples of what may be termed the cavern style of domestic architecture, as their darkness tempered by inartificial chinks, together with their free exhibition of undisguised stone and earth in walls and flooring, suggest a cave-dwelling in almost its severe primæval rudeness. The Pat Ryans' does so in a marked degree, perhaps because its most prominent articles of furniture are the two long rough tree-trunks, dug out of the bog in the progress of some season's turf-cutting, which serve the family for seats. The master of the house, sitting pensively on the end of one of them, might now, with the accessories of a few flint-axes, celts, and an uncanny-looking lizard or two, have posed well enough as his own geological ancestor dating from some abysmal palæolithic or preglacial period.

Presently Pat raised his head and remarked in an injured tone : "Arrah now, Denny, I wish you'd lave jobbin' one in the leg that-a way. I declare I thought it was a horsefly was on me."

Denis Ryan, who was very fat and about three years old, only grinned nearly all round his head, and said triumphantly : " Molly, Molly—I'm after stickin' father wid the handle o' me spoo-an." Whereupon something smaller and still fatter began to crawl rapidly over the floor, evidently with designs of participating in this detectable amusement.

"Och, bad manners to you childer, can't you let the man ait his bit o' food in paice?" said their mother in remonstrant appeal. "Here's your own dinners just ready, if you'd settle down to it conformable, and quit annoyin' other people."

"Oh, for that matter, I'm finished," said Pat, getting up; "I was on'y waitin' till the flurry o' the win' was gone by a bit to step down and fetch in the tools from where we were workin' yisterday. Tom had a right to ha' brought them in, but he went off at all hours along wid Ody Rafferty and th' ould ass."

"He did so," said Mrs. Pat, "and I wonder, be the same token, what at all took them in the sthrames of rain. I hope to goodness he'll not be landin' himself in the middle of some great ould botheration before he's done."

"How should—ah—I know?" said Pat, swallowing a rainy gust as he crossed the threshold. "Begob, Hughey Quigley's scrapeen of oats looks as if seven mad bullocks had been rowlin' themselves in it. Divil recaive the straw of it'll ever stand up on its right end in this world. Sure, except to be raisin' yourself ruination and desthruc—" The rest of the sentence went over the bog on a keening blast.

About the same time, the Kilfoyles next door were talking over their dinner. The Kilfoyles' cabin was at one period an object which caught the eye of everybody who came into Lisconnel, and though much toned down and subdued, it even now presents a rather distinguished appearance. For one day Thady, the lad who used to bring his mother little packets of tea and sugar, until he unhappily had his skull fractured by a kicking cart-horse down below on Hilfirthy's farm, took it into his head to do a job of whitewashing, and carried up a creelful of lumps of lime from Classon's kiln. These he slaked in an old washing-tub, still ruefully referred to by Mrs. Brian as being "fit for nothin' else from that good hour to this," and splashed away with a lavishness which atoned for want of skill, or any handier brush than a besom of dried broom and heather. In his thoroughgoingness he whitened the very turf-stack, and looked longingly at the moss-rusted thatch. In consequence, for several months afterwards the snowy walls gleamed conspicuously on the black bogland far and wide; and though that was years ago, and smoke within and rain without have been busily effacing Thady's handiwork, traces of it still linger, especially on the east end, turned away from the weather, and in sheltered angles under the eaves. Moreover, incited by a consciousness of their remarkable exterior, the Kilfoyles sought to improve upon it by bounding themselves on two sides with an elaborate fence, not a mere ordinary stone dyke. This remains to the present day, and is composed of materials which, save for the charm of variety, do not strike you as superior to those commonly in use. Worn-out kettles and pots are among them, and old boxes, and fragments of wrecked carts, mixed with battered tins and cannisters, and such other *débris* of civilisation as we see tossed up on its remotest verge, looking as incongruous and unaccountable there as the husks and shells of tropical fruits washed in with the slimy green ooze and brown trailing wrack on a northern beach.

Nothwithstanding all this external elegance, however, the Kilfoyles fare no more sumptuously than the rest of Lisconnel, and were looking forward quite as eagerly to their new potatoes. In his speculations thereupon, Brian, who had gone further a-harvesting than most of his neighbours, and abounded in travellers' tales, was led to mention a wonderful machine, which a man had told him another man had actually seen somewhere at work. "A most surprisin' little affair of a yoke, wid twisted wheels to it, that dhrud along aisy, and just whirreld the pitaties up out o' the ground afore they knew where they were."

Mrs. Brian was of the opinion that she'd liefer not have any such a thing meddlin' or makin' wid her pitaties. It might be a great conthrivance, but somehow to roke them out that way wholesale seemed onnatural like. To which her husband responded: "Sure, accordin' to that gait o'goin,' it's onnatural to turn them up wid a graip or a spade; we'd a right to be lavin' them sittin' paiceable in their dhrills. Or, bedad, they mightn't ever happen to get planted at all at all, onless it's natural to be sliverin' them in slices, and stickin' them down in thrinches. I dunno how you're goin' to manage it," said Brian, who found, like other controversialists, that his argument was beginning to demonstrate cumbrously large facts. So he shunted himself on to another line and continued: "'Twould have to be a cliver divil of a machine, what you might call rael injanious, before 'twould whirrel a many pitaties out o' some o' those dhrills of ours. There's a terrible dale of them missed on us in odd places—bad cess to it—'twas them blamed late frosts in Aperl."

Everybody looked grave at that hearing, and saw inwardly a picture of the dark-green rows marred by gaps, uglier eyesores for Lisconnel than for the bibliomaniac the blanks in his shelves which signify a broken set.

"The saints send it may turn out a better crop than last year's," said Mrs. Brian, "for a body does git fairly sickened wid the long spell of this stuff we're after havin.' Goodness forgive me for grumblin' agin' it—but it's haythinish it is; and it comes hard on the childer, poor crathurs. Tim, jewel, stop where you are, and don't be inticin' the rest of them to folly you out under the pours of rain. Sure, I'm heart-scalded wid bilin' it—weary on it—you might keep it on the fire till the latter end of Doomsday, and sorra a taste o' goodness there'd been in it when ye'd done."

"Why sure, Norah me dear," piped little old Mrs. Kilfoyle, wishing to please, "this is grand male you got last time—better than common. I was thinkin' to git a sort of flaviour of oaten-male off of it."

"Look-a Norah, me mother's ready for another bit," said Brian, gratified, but misunderstanding her.

"Och to gracious, no lad," protested his mother, while his wife began to run the big iron spoon vigorously round the pot. "Is it choked yous 'ud be havin' me all out?" And she took refuge in the doorway, towards which the flaw-blown puddles outside seemed to make incessant short rushes, invariably baulked by some unseen impediment. "It's worser the day's gittin'," she remarked. "There's young Pat Ryan goin' down the bog, and a blast's narely riz him off his feet."

Then she said: "God save you, Mrs. M'Gurk; you're abroad in great auld polthers. Stand in wid yourself, ma'am, out o' the win'."

"It's not too bad between the showers," said the widow M'Gurk, standing in, "and I was after slippin' down to Mrs. Sheridan's wid the pig's bucket"—this was, strictly speaking, an old hot-water can. "Eh, Brian, man alive, how's yourself? It's quare weather we're gittin'; what d'you say to it at all? Did you happin to notice Hughey Quigley's oats this mornin'? They're just a livin' wisp o' disthruction. You might as well think to be puttin' a rapin-hook into the ravels of an ould rag mat. And it doin' so finely until the rain got lambastin' it."

"Ay bedad, and himself as sot up wid it as could be conceived," said Mrs. Kilfoyle; "and small blame to him, poor man, for 'twas lookin' lovely, that smooth and greeny."

"It's the sort of colour one might fancy a linin' of to one's eyes," said Mrs. Brian, rubbing her own, which the turf-smoke made smart.

"'Twas a dacintish little strip," Brian said, "but sure the man was a great fool to go plant the like. He might ha' known 'twould merely be disthroyed on him. There's nothin' to aquil the win' and the wet for devastatin' all before them, when they get colloguin' together."

"I'm sure I dunno what plisure Anybody," said Mrs. M'Gurk, secretly attaching a definite idea to her indefinite pronoun, "can take in ruinatin' a poor person's bit o' property. If I was one, now, that had the mindin' of such things, and took notice of a little green field sittin' in the black o' the bog, it's apter I'd be to let it have its chanst, at any rate, to ripen itself the best way it could, than go for to sluice the great dowses of rain on top of it, and lave it all battered and bet into flittherjigs like yon."

"'Deed then, it's a pity to behould, so it is," said Mrs. Kilfoyle, "and as for plisure, I see no signs of plisure in it for anybody good or bad. It's liker a sort of accident to my notion. Such a thing might happen ready enough, if you come to considher the power o' wet there does be streelin' about promiscuous over our heads. Sure them that has the conthroulin' of it might aisy slop down a sup too much of it on some little place widout any harrum' intendin', the same as you might be after doin' yourself when you're fillin'. a weeny jug out of a big can. I wouldn't wonder now if that was the way of it: just an accident like, and no thoughts of ruinatin' anythin'."

"It maybe might be," said Mrs. M'Gurk, staring ruefully through the thick-quivering strands of rain, and apparently not much consoled by Mrs.

Kilfoyle's teleology. "But bedad 'twould make a great differ to the likes of us, if they'd be a trifle more exact."

"I dunno," said Mrs. Kilfoyle. "I'm none so sure it mightn't give one the idee that they had set their minds to managin' such-like consarns for us because it was the on'y thing for us they could be doin' at all. And that 'ud be a poor case. I'd a dale liefer think they were took up wid conthrivin' us somethin' better. Och, woman dear, if you had the grandest crops that ever grew, they wouldn't hinder you takin' thought of them you'll see goin' about your fields no more while you're left in this world."

"Bedad no," said the widow M'Gurk.

"I'd chance it," said poor Mrs. Brian, whose children were all alive, and if possible to be kept so.

"D'ye see that there?" Brian said, crooking his thumb at a place where the rain had bored a new passage through the straw and scraws, and was ticking down rhythmically in large slow sooty drops, like a self-constituted clepsydra; "it's my belief the whole countryside's settled under a dhrip, the same as that bit o' flure, so there's no sinse in findin' fau't wid any one for not keepin' it dhry." Brian looked cheered up by his little conceit, but the three women gazed rather blankly at the plashing drop, as if they had been referred to, and were studying, a difficult solution of the problem.

They were interrupted by a summons from without, as peremptory-sounding as a sudden clatter of hail on your window-pane: "Mrs. Brian—Mrs. Brian—Mrs. Brian, ma'am." Mrs. Quigley, who lived nearly opposite to the Kilfoyles, was calling from over the wet way, very audibly exasperated. "I'll throuble you, ma'am, to speak to your Tim there. He's just after slappin' a big sod o' turf over the dyke into the middle of me chuckens, that went as nare doin' slaughther on the half of them as ever I saw. The crathurs were that terrified, I give you me word they lep up ten fut standin' off of the ground."

Chuckens are in Lisconnel an occasionally convenient cause of war, hostilities being sometimes commenced by an ostentatious sweeping out at your door of a neighbour's vagrant brood, which, when things were on a peace establishment, would have pervaded the mud-floor and pecked futilely for worms among the turf-sods unforbidden.

The nine white fluff-balls which represented Mrs. Quigley's chuckens, had, however, recovered from their alarm and phenomenal acrobatic exertions, and were bobbing about on the black mould under the feet of a high-stepping fatuously solemn fawn-coloured hen.

"Tim," quoth Mrs. Brian to a cluster of huddled-together heads, which were designing broken-crockery works among the puddles at a short distance, "you'll sup sorrow wid a spoon of grief if I hear of your doin' anythin' agin to Mrs. Quigley's chuckens."

And therewith the incident would have terminated amicably, Tim being happily indifferent to the prospect of that often threatened repast, had not Mrs. Quigley's still vibrating wrath moved her to say, addressing nobody in particular: "Begob, it's a quare way some people has of bringin' up their childer to be mischievous little pests, whatever they get to meddlin' wid."

Of course such a pointed thrust had to be parried, so Mrs. Brian at once bawled with very distinct enunciation: "Tim, Tim, come in out of that, there's a good boy, and bring Norah and Biddy along wid you. *You've* got dacint rags of clothes on· you to be spoilt wid the wet, not the scandeelious ould scarecrow dudeens that some I could name think good enough to be makin' shows of their childer in."

I doubt myself but that an unbiassed judge would have pronounced the respective wardrobes of the young Quigleys and young Kilfoyles to be much on a par; however, Mrs. Quigley took the observation as it was meant, and rejoined: "Well, then, it's lucky for them if they've got anythin' dacint about them at all; for what else they're like to be gettin' where they come from excipt ignorince and impidence is more than I can say."

The rising up of a quarrel in Lisconnel is often as abrupt as the descent of a squall on a mountain lake; so it was quite in the nature of such things that Mrs. Brian's next retort should be uncompromising in tone: "Och, and is it talkin' you are of ignorince and imperince? Be the piper, if it was that sort I was a-wantin', I'd know right well were to go look for them, so long as there was one of the Quigleys anywheres around."

Then Mrs. Quigley said: "It's not throublin' meself I am to be answerin' the likes of yous." And Mrs. M'Gurk said: "Maybe if you'd the sinse, you'd be plased to git the chanst of spakin' to respectable people." And Mrs. Quigley said: "Respectable *how are you?*" a phrase fraught in Lisconnel with the most blighting sarcasm, and added that it would be a thankful mercy if some ould women could lave interfarin' in other people's consarns alone. And then Mrs. M'Gurk and Mrs. Brian simultaneously requested one another to listen to the fine gabbin' she was havin' out of her that day. As for old little Mrs. Kilfoyle, who loved peace, and whose frail thread of voice could not, in any case, have availed much in an engagement carried on at so long a range, she only clacked softly to herself like a discomfited blackbird, and ever and anon admonished her friends to come in wid themselves and never mind argufying; while her son Brian, sitting serenely aloof from the fray, intimated to her by knowing winks and grimaces his masculine disdain for such a strife of tongues, in which, however, he was agreeably aware that his wife could efficiently uphold the family cause.

The road at this place is of considerable width, broad enough to accommodate across it a system of five or six puddles of ample size, and the wind ruffling straight down it, although like an honest umpire inclining to neither belligerent, did whisk away the point of some scathingly hurled epigrams, in a manner which helped to discourage both parties. Mrs. Quigley had, on the whole, the worst of it, which was no disgrace to her, seeing that she had been obliged to quit the shelter of her eaves in order to come within screeching distance, and had, moreover, fought single-handed, since "Himself," although at home, remained supinely indoors, and only gave her the meagre moral support derivable from fitful muffled bellows, which might have meant almost anything. But the sharpness of the contention may be inferred from the fact that when, routed ostensibly by a heavier downpour, she scuttered off towards her dwelling, the last utterance which she gave to the wet winds was: "May the divil sail away wid the half of yous;" and that the next blast bore, rather beyond its mark, the antiphonal response: "And may he sail away wid *you, too*, ma'am."

Lisconnel soaked on undisturbed and unenlivened for some time after this, but it was destined to have two more sensations before the day finally closed in. The sun had imperceptibly sunk, and it was raining harder than ever, "most ungovernably," Hughey Quigley said, when all at once something happened in the western sky. It was as if some vast tent-rope had suddenly been snapped, for the dark riftless cloud-canopy seemed not so much to abruptly rise as to actually recoil back with a swing up from the horizon's verge, and ere one had well realised that it had begun to lift, it was flying eastward, scudding in festoons and trails and shreds, or furled into rumpled bundles in the grip of the careering blasts. It left behind it spaces of marvellously limpid lough-blue and sea-green, just deep enough for the present to drown out the stars; and low along the dusky purple earth-rim the sun's fiery wake was still traced through a haze as of amber-seething foam. Reflections of this were caught glimmeringly in shallow pools, or on the wet faces of rocks, superseding the twilight with a dim golden radiance, which stole over the landscape like the fitting sequel to a gorgeous sundown. Five minutes after the first rent in the clouds, Lisconnel looked as if it had been basking all day under the beams of a stainless heaven, and might count upon spending the morrow in the same fashion. These rapid transformations are not of rare occurrence here among wide levels and open sky-reaches, where the wild west wind is a very deft scene-shifter ; however, so little else does happen, and so much generally depends upon the weather, that their repetition seldom falls flat. Now everybody looked out interestedly, and said that the evening seemed holding up a bit; and thus it chanced that several persons descried Ody Rafferty, ass, and comrade, returning sooner than had been expected, and by an unusual route, across the bog.

Ody Rafferty is a man of whom his acquaintances say: " Och, bedad, it's himself's the ould boys that's in it." Their tone when thus summing up his character is half self-congratulatory and half envious, as if they felt that the ability to duly appreciate the extreme wiliness of him was in itself something—as much, perhaps, as they could lawfully wish—and yet did leave them something unattainable to desire. I am not aware that he has ever performed any feat remarkable enough to justify their excessively high opinion of his shrewdness, and I fancy that his reputation is one of those which are secure against overthrow because they rest upon nothing in particular.

He lived at this time in the cabin which stands back from the road near the O'Driscolls' ruins, and he had lately become the owner of a small turf-coloured ass, rather to the disgust of some neighbours, who found her energetic grazing trench upon the limited browsing-grounds of their goats. Their dissatisfaction, however, was abated by the knowledge of the uses for which he kept the beast, no secret at Lisconnel, though etiquette prescribed its treatment as such. That knowledge made everybody eager to learn why he had brought his *load of turf* round by the back of the ridge, instead of straight across the strip between it and the road; but Ody did not choose to satisfy their curiosity. He had in truth made the *détour* for reasons which he could have no possible object in concealing, but, as if his redundant guile sought for supererogatory works, he enveloped the fact in a veil of mystery, which by satyr-like leers and grins he admonished his companions, Tom Ryan and young O'Beirne, not to lift. He himself set them the example of baffling inquiries with the evasive answers fashionable among us, such as: " Och, that's the chat now," or "There's where the night fell on you," or "Begob, if you knew that and had your supper, you might go to bed."

This reticent attitude he maintained inexorably all the way to the top of the hill, for they were only passing through Lisconnel, their destination being Dan O'Beirne's, near Duffclane; and if I know Ody, he thoroughly enjoyed his progress, as he stumped along beside his meek Jinny, saying blandly, "Git on, ould woman, we must be steppin' it," whenever his escorting friends waxed particularly urgent and eager in their questioning. But when the knockawn lay behind them, and the neighbours had dropped off discontentedly, he called his sons Paddy and Luke, who were still following, and bade them run home and bid their mother to be looking out for him about noon the next day. "And yous may tell her, lads," he added, "that if we hadn't went round back of the risin' ground, we'd ha' got bogged up to the neck wid the swamps there do be all about where the sthrame's after over-flowin' itself. And look-a Paddy, if you've the wit, you might be tellin' her that the raison we come home to-day instead of to-morra was because themselves over beyant had took a notion they'd a chanst of resaivin' company prisently, and were wishful to git the place readied up and clared out in a manner beforehand. Sure one must humour the women a bit," he explained to Tom and young O'Beirne. "The wife 'ud be as onaisy as an ould hin on a hot griddle all the while I was gone, if she didn't think she knew the rights of it."

"Me sister-in-law was rael mad that I wouldn't be tellin' her," Tom Ryan said complacently—"leppin' she was."

"Let her lep," said Ody.

CHAPTER V.

GOT THE BETTER OF.

IT seems advisable to explain without further delay the nature of Ody Rafferty's calling, lest some hints which have been dropped should mislead you into supposing Lisconnel implicated in transactions more nefarious than is really the case. Nor could I otherwise fulfil a half-promise to relate what became of his ass Jinny. The truth, briefly stated, is that he employed her in conveying earthenware jars of potheen from a certain wholly illicit still off away in the bog to O'Beirne the blacksmith's forge near Duffclane, an establishment which I fear must be described as little better than a shebeen. Happily it is not necessary for me, in a plain narrative of facts, to pass judgment upon Ody's actions, or to inquire whether it be an extenuating or an aggravating circumstance that he committed them more for the pleasure of the incidental excitement, than for the sake of any pecuniary profits thence accruing, which were indeed very small. For although this still, which I believe continues to prosper, turns out many gallons of the rael crathur, few of them flow towards Duffclane. Most of them go, in the first instance, on board quaint little *curraghs* and *pookawns*, stationed in sundry creeks and inlets, and thus arrive at various villages along the nookshotten coast, as far as to Kenport itself. Ody's carrying trade was therefore done on a limited scale, and sometimes hardly made good the expense of Jinny's keep, if he had regarded the matter from a purely business point of view. But he valued it chiefly as a congenial pursuit giving scope to his acknowledged cuteness and a stirring spirit of enterprise, which made more everyday avocations irksome to him. His long family supplied much more labour than was needed for the cultivation of his bit o' land and the cutting of his turf; and albeit he entertained but an humble opinion of its members' intelligence, he willingly entrusted them with the execution of those humdrum tasks, and gave himself to higher things. He found all the details of the undertaking more or less enjoyable. Each successfully accomplished transit of the wild bog-tract was for him pervaded with a flattering sense of having "got the better of" somebody— a thing he loved to do—and each arrival, mostly in the moth-coloured dusk, at the black mouth of Dan O'Beirne's scarlet-hearted forge was a triumphant moment to be anticipated from afar.

The way he went is long and monotonous enough to need some such inward enlivening. I have never ascertained the site of the still with any accuracy, just knowing vaguely that to get there you strike out into the bog northward from Lisconnel, and proceed until its surface begins to heave and fall in undulations which fore-run the mountainous coast-line. Even much minuter directions would scarcely guide one to the intricately situated shieling, which doubtless seems the innocent turf-bank, and only by a faint puff of blue smoke betrays the worm beneath. But it must be a full day's journey distant, when that journey is measured by the gingerly steps of a little ass ; and to spend a whole day in profitably breaking the law and defiantly defrauding the revenue was worth a great deal of trudging. Ody Rafferty did not, however, run by any means so many risks as might have been expected on these journeys, nor were his strategical abilities, after all, put into much requisition. This is clear from the fact that for several years he habitually brought his potheen over the bog and along the Duffclane road under the transparently inartificial pretence of convoying a load of turf. Now, no rational person could seriously suppose Dan O'Beirne in the least likely to send a matter of twenty miles for the fuel which grew at his door; and therefore it may be assumed that anybody who was taken in by the device, was so with his own good will. Indeed, except for the name of the thing, as people whispered at Lisconnel, Ody might almost as well have forborne to pile up the brown-fibred sods over the paler drab jars, whose contents any one who chose might have heard gurgling as they were joggled along. However, the omission would have slightly diminished his own gratification, and increased the embarrassments of Sergeant Boyd.

The truth is that Duffclane at this time was, constabularily speaking, under the charge of a very portly and placid King Log. Sergeant Boyd and the four or five subordinates who shared with him the whitewashed iron police-hut erected on the shore of the little rushy-ended lough near the village, were as unaggressive, easy-going a set of men as you could wish to see patrolling in couples at the regulation rate, or, more commonly, sitting, in the face of all regulations with the solace of a pipe, on some wayside bank or wall. And, as such, they found in Duffclane quarters greatly to their mind; so much so, that once when they were accidentally overlooked by the authorities at the season of periodical shiftings, and left unremoved, they entered no protest against the blunder, but stayed on unrepiningly at the back of beyant, to the satisfaction of all parties concerned.

Easily though he went, however, the sergeant liked a little conviviality as well as other people, and not seldom put in an appearance at the forge of an evening, when Dan O'Beirne's club had gathered about his glowing flame-bank, often the most cheering feature in the landscape for many a mirky mile round. On these occasions nobody with a spark of honourable feeling beneath his invisible-green tunic would have dreamed of making the remotest allusion to the antecedents of the fragrant amber-brown "dhrop" which was sure to be forthcoming in a thick-lipped glass; and indeed nothing could have appeared further from Sergeant Boyd's wishes. It is said that once when Ody Rafferty, by an untoward mishap, let a full gallon jar slip off Jinny's back from among the deceptive sods, and smash itself on a stone, actually splashing the sergeant's boots with its criminating contents, the sergeant instantly turned and fled away down the road at the double, " as if he heard high thrason, and blue murdher, and ivery sort of divarsion you plase, yellyhooin' for him round the corner." But I cannot certify the truth of this anecdote.

Of course this state of things could not continue

indefinitely. Burly Sergeant Boyd departed to another station, taking with him the character (unofficial) of a dacint, good-natured man; and his successor was of a different type. Acting-Sergeant Clarke had an aspiring mind, and was athirst for distinction. He dreamed sometimes of a District-Inspectorship, and then always awoke with strong views as to the expediency of repressing crime. Now at remote little Duffclane the one field which gives any promise of materials for a creditable monthly report is the shebeening by Sergeant Boyd so wilfully ignored. Alert and experienced, the new officer was quick to grasp the fact, and to perceive signs that the unlawful pursuit had long been followed in the district on a somewhat extensive scale, and with an audacity fostered by his predecessor's remissness, if not connivance. Accordingly he lost no time in casting about for the means of promptly effecting an important seizure, which might prove a short cut to promotion. Thenceforth in imaginative meditations he continually saw himself upsetting tubs of seething wash, confiscating plant, and marching disconcerted prisoners over the bog to the nearest barracks. Tidings of this regrettable change made their way in due course to Lisconnel. But Sergeant Clarke knew better than to display any overt activity, and at first the rumours ran dimly to the effect that "the new lot down below at the polis-hut were quare ould ones, and noways to be depinded upon." The resultant danger had come, as we shall see, very close indeed, before it took a clearer shape.

One mackerel-skied September afternoon, Ody Rafferty halted at his own door on his way to O'Beirne's, and annoyed his wife a good deal by letting Jinny the ass drink up a bucketful of water, which she had just fetched from a neighbouring pool. Ody had by this time owned Jinny for nearly three years, and had conceived an extraordinary high opinion of her.

"I declare to goodness the figurandyin' you have wid that baste," Mrs. Rafferty protested, "bangs all. Couldn't you as well ha' been givin' her a dhrink out of the water goin' by it, instead of settin' her to gulp up the sup I was after gettin' to put the pitaties in? It's disgustin' to see you makin' a fool of her as if she was a human crathur." Ody, indeed, had a habit of disadvantageously contrasting his family's faculties, mental and moral, with those of Jinny, which perhaps added a tang of bitterness to his wife's tone. He now said: "Be the hokey, it's herself has more gumption and comperhinsion in her than the half of yous all rowled together. She's not the fool, anyway, to be dhrinkin' out o' wather-pools thick wid them black wather-asks, that 'ud lep down your throath as soon as look at you—and that's what Maryanne and Jim and the rest of them's after this minyit—I noticed them coming along." This, as Ody may have expected, sent his wife speeding off to drag away the children from those reptilian perils, and he continued: "Molly there, stir your stumps, and run to be pullin' her a few wisps of the long grass under the dyke, afore we're jiggin' on agin."

But Molly did not run. For at this moment Paddy, a younger brother, bolted in among them with awful tidings. The new sergeant and a pair of strange constables were about a couple of miles down the Duffclane road, hiding out of sight behind some furze-bushes and clumps of broom, to wait for some people and an ass coming by. Paddy had slipped near them unbeknownst, and had gathered this much from their discourse; whereupon, being, despite his father's disparagements, not devoid of mother-wit, he had skyted home at full speed to intercept and warn the destined victims of the ambuscade.

Ody was very loth to accept this sinister report, partly because it augured so ill for the future prospects of his trade, and partly because, if it were true, he had been saved from a snare by a person of mental gifts far inferior to his own, which to some minds is ever a harrowing admission, not to be smoothed over by any applications of the Lion and the Mouse—an apologue with which Ody, however, was not probably acquainted. He sought consequently to postpone the evil moment of conviction by pronouncing Paddy's story not only incredible, but incomprehensible, and continued to asseverate with heat that he'd divil a bit of a notion what the bosthoon was blatherin' there about, until his wife, his daughter, Tom Ryan, and Mrs. M'Gurk had each severally rehearsed the statement to him, succinctly and clearly enough to preclude further persistence in that subterfuge.

"Och, well then," he said at last, reluctantly and tacitly abandoning his sceptical attitude, "what did you say them chaps were exactually doin' the time you come away?"

"A-sittin' in a hape under the hollow o' the bank," quoth Paddy, "passin' the remark that them lads might be comin' along any time now. The fat-faced one did be slippin' two sixpenny-bits and a shillin' in and out of his pocket, and him wid the black whiskers had somethin' aitin'—cheese it might be. But just the last thing, the sergeant he ups and cocks his chin agin' the top-edge of the bank, and was squintin' through the furze-bush with the little eyes of him like an ould ferret; and sez he, 'We've a grand view down a sthretch of the road from this, so as we can stip over convanient and stop them afore they know where they've got to. And manewhile,' sez he, wid a great dirty grin on his face, ' we're as agreeable here as need be, and not cramped up the way we was that time at the bridge,' sez he. So I legged it off wid meself, and there I left them—divil sweep them all."

"I'd love to be throwin' stones and clay at them," said Molly Rafferty, meditatively.

"Begorrah then, I'll be very apt to be givin' them a clout on the head, if they thry interfaring wid *me*," said Tom Ryan, who was Ody Rafferty's confederate on this day's expedition.

The sentiment was approved by all the gossoons of any size—and some of extremely little—who were within hearing. Many of them capered and said, "Hurrooh—to your sowls!" and others plucked Tom's ragged sleeves, saying in hoarse whispers, "Let's come along then—ah, do now!" The cropped heads rapidly sorted themselves from the shawled ones, and converged as if something drew them towards a centre, while the women and girls began to stand round with open mouths and eyes. In short, Lisconnel got up the symptoms of a miniature rising with a creditable celerity, considering that nearly all its able-bodied men were away harvesting down below. A person who still wore petticoats, and was not yet fully five years old, might have been heard to remark with confidence, " Sure, we'll dhrive the pack of them before us " ; but Ody Rafferty was of an age to recognise all this as wildness.

" Och ! git along wid you, Tom," he said, " and whisht talkin' foolish about cloutin' the pólis. It's no thing to go do, onless you're put to it entirely. We'll git the better of thim yit, one way or the other, but it won't be by walkin' sthraight down their threacherous throaths, which is what they're intindin'. I'll just be unloadin' me sods and things off of the poor ass, and let her git her bit o' grazin' in paice. She'll go no further this evenin'—the back o' me hand to the lot o' them. The boys below 'ill have to do widout their dhrop to-night, if they're depindin' on me. . . . One of yous just run up the hill," he commanded, when Jinny was nearly unladen, " and be keepin' a look-out down the road, for 'fraid them thieves of mischief might happen to come slingein' in on top of us. And then I'll take and slip me couple of jars in among the growth of rooshes under the edge—Och! no, you great gomeral, not there, to be starin' out, you may say, at every one goin' the road—the edge of the hole over there alongside of the big stack. It's none too deep, and they'll lie there handy till we git another chanst. Lave liftin' them, Biddy ; don't any of yous be meddlin' wid them *at all*

Musha, long life to th' ould sergeant; I hope he'll git his health this night till he sees us comin' by!"

It was Stacey Doyne who hindered the carrying out of these prudent plans. While the whiskey-jars were still lying at the Raffertys' door, she ran up in great dismay. Lisconnel had gone through a season of sickness, the early summer fasts having been followed by an outbreak of fever, from an attack of which Stacey's mother was recovering. But she remained very low and feeble, and this evening had been "taking wakenesses" in a manner which frightened her daughter out of her wits. "I dunno what to be at wid her," said Stacey, "she's that wake like, and never a bit of a thing can I persuade her to touch. I've tried her wid the sup o' milk Mrs. M'Gurk gave me, and a drink of fresh water, and a wee taste of a malcy pitaty—and that's all I have; but she won't so much as look at them. I'm afeard she's rael bad; and the lads away on us down below. So when I saw all of yous up here, I just took a run out to tell you the way she was." Stacey was so miserably anxious and scared, that all the lines which would be fixed on her face a dozen years hence came out, as invisible writing does at a flame, and made its youth haggard. All her neighbours commiserated, and said, "Ah, the crathur!"—but Ody Rafferty had something more practical to offer.

"I'll tell you what it is," he said, taking up one of the jars; "it's a sup of this your mother wants, and a sup of this she'll git. Norah, woman, run in and fetch th'ould cork-screwer out of the press, and bring a mug or somethin' along. . . . You'll just make her swally a good dhrop of that, Stacey, like it or no, and you'll soon see she'll be the better for it. Och, bedad, it's not a right Irishwoman she'd be if she a-wouldn't. Look, now, at the colour of that; there's an eye of the sun glamin' through it. She'll feel herself able enough for her bit of hot pitaty wunst you've heartened her up that way—aitin' all before her she'll be; and the next thing we hare tell of her, she'll be dancin' jigs like a three-year-old. Musha, sure the strongest person iver stepped will be takin' a bad turn now and agin. Just run away home wid it to her, Stacey, jewel, and don't be frettin' yourself, for there's no fear but she'll over it finely in next to no time, plase the Lord."

"God reward you, Ody Rafferty," said Stacey, with the fervent gratitude which we feel towards any one who loosens the grip on us of a torturing fear; for she was as much reassured by his flow of eloquence as by the possession of the purple-speckled delft pint-mug, tucked away carefully under a corner of her shawl. "May the blessin' of Heaven above shine on you! Faith, it's prayin' for you all I'll be to the last day of me life, it it does her a benefit."

Then Stacey hurried home; and as most of the neighbours went off with her to superintend the administration of Ody's remedy, or to prescribe others of their own, there was no visible reason why he should not have proceeded to fulfil his intentions respecting the jars of potheen. Reasons, indeed, were perhaps afloat on the air in the form of microscope-baffling particles; but whether or no, what followed certainly tends to confirm the truth of a saying we have at Lisconnel: that it's a dale aisier to draw the cork out of a full bottle of whiskey than to put it in agin.

"Tom," said Ody, as the patter of the bare feet died away, and nothing was heard save the rhythmical munches of Jinny browsing between the furze-bushes, "we'd find somethin' handier for taking a sup out of, if we stepped inside."

When, some three-quarters of an hour later, Mrs. Rafferty came home with the report that Mrs. Doyne was finding herself a good trifle stronger, she at once perceived what had taken place. Tom Ryan, a weak-headed youth, was far past making any pretence of keeping up appearances. He simply sat leaning against the wall near the door, and hardly woke up sufficiently to say, between violent nods, "Aw—whaw?" when addressed sarcastically as "An iligant spicimin, sittin' there lookin' about as sinsible as an ould blind cow caught in a shower o' hail." Ody, on the contrary, seemed even more wide-awake and sententious than usual. Yet his wife, who knew his ways, viewed him with suspicions which proved not unfounded. At first, however, only a few casual remarks passed between them. Then he rose, clapped down the cork of the opened jar with the palm of his hand, and said: "It's time for me to be steppin'."

"Is it puttin' them away you'd be?" inquired Mrs. Rafferty. "Time it is for that, bedad."

"I dunno what you may call puttin' them away. I'm a-goin' to take of this one, that has nary a sup out of it, along down to the pólis-hut at Duffclane, if that's what you mane."

"The great goodness deliver us, Ody! what was that you were sayin'?"

"Didn't I say it plain? Is it stupid the woman's grown? To the pólis-hut, I said. Wasn't that gomeral Paddy up here awhile ago with the order? Somethin' he said about lavin' it down at the turn of the road for themselves to be fetchin' it home, but likely that was just a botch he was makin' of the matter. That's no way to be deliverin' of goods. It's to their door I'll bring it dacint, and morebetoken ped for it I'll be afore I quit. A gallon of as grand stuff as iver was poured in a glass. It's somethin', bejabers, to be the pólis these times, givin' their orders for what's a long sight too good for the likes o' them. Howane'er, their money's no worser than respectable people's."

Mrs. Rafferty stood aghast, discerning full well what had befallen. Among the most mischievous and unmanageable effects of "drink taken," is the supervening in the patient of some fixed hallucination, which leaves his general faculties unimpaired, or rather furbished up and whetted to aid him ruinously in pursuing whatever demented line of conduct his delusion may dictate. To this affection Ody was upon occasion subject, and it now appeared that his potations of the strong new whiskey had already conjured up in his mind a grotesque figment, which derived its substance from Paddy's story of the police ambuscade, distorted out of all shape into a phantom uncannily well adapted for inveigling him straight into the trap. A will-o'-the-wisp luring him over the bog with its goblin glede could scarcely land him in a more critical position than his would be should he present himself at the barracks, or the place where the police lay in wait, with a gallon of potheen avowedly in his possession. And such a fate he was evidently resolved to court. Experience had taught Mrs. Rafferty that under these circumstances to argue or remonstrate was very bootless; so she could but look blankly from one daughter's face to the other's, and in neither found any more counsel or comfort than in the spectacle of Tom's witlessly bobbing head. Her husband began, with cheerful whistling, to adjust and tighten the hay-bands wound above the tops of his wrinkled brogues.

"Boys," she said in a solemn whisper to a pair of small Rafferty gossoons, who were at the door, "run and huroosha th'ould ass a bit down the bog, afore he comes out. She's grazin there behind the stack—'Twill delay him awhile hoontin' and catchin' her," she continued, transferring the whisper to her girls; but they all felt it was only a desperate and temporary expedient.

"Look at that objick now," said Ody, pausing at the door to eye Tom's collapse with calm disdain, "one might suppose he was after takin' the full of Lough Inagh. You'd better just dowse a pail of water over him, and let him wake up and rowl home."

"And how are you goin' to manage along wid on'y yourself and the ass?" insinuated Mrs. Rafferty, catching at a last straw.

"Aisy. You haven't the sinse to comperhind that when you're doin' jobs for the bastely pólis, you've no need of anybody runnin' on ahead to look round corners and the like. Whisht gabbin', woman alive, and don't be showin' off your ignorince." He left his wife crushed, though not in the way he imagined.

Ody had to spend a considerable time in catching Jinny, as the boys had done their hurooshing with much enthusiasm. He returned from the pursuit in an ill humour, which he vented by accusing his family of having moved the whiskey jars on the table, and he stowed away the partially empty one in a recess by the hearth, breathing out grim threats of vengeance should he find that anybody had meddled with it during his absence. Perhaps, too, his racing, and scrambling, and shouting at Jinny's coquettishly flourished heels, had slightly confused his ideas. At any rate, the bystanders exchanged significant glances, when they saw him carefully fasten a single small turf-sod over the jar tied on the ass's back, a proceeding absurd considered as a ruse, and furthermore inconsistent with his own account of his errand. Little Luke Quigley, a daring spirit, whose mother was continually exhorting him, in admiring accents, not to be a bold boy, ventured to inquire: "And did the pólis order that grand loadin' of turf from you too, Ody Rafferty?" But Ody held imperturbably on his way, if anything less crab-gaited than usual, and with a preternaturally knowing expression. "You might as well have attempted to turn back the sun in the sky," his wife said, as she ruefully watched him over the hill.

By sunset that evening the air had grown misty and chilly, and the police party down at the bend of the road had begun to weary of their long watch. Constable M'Kenna had left off jingling his loose coins, and was listlessly shelling furze-seeds; Constable Flynn had finished his bread and cheese; and Sergeant Clarke found it harder and harder to keep his mind patiently fixed on the important disclosures which would probably result from the capture of this convoy. They observed at ever shorter intervals: "They had a right to ha' been here by now;" but nothing appeared except the dusk, and at last the sergeant said: "Accordin' to informations, I made sure they'd be passin' along this way to-night; but there'd be no use stayin' where we are after dark, for they'd not be likely to leave themselves that late startin' from the place above. We'll just chance it—Flynn, do you go cautious as far as the lump of rock yonder, and see if there's a sign of anything coming further up the road. If there's not, we may as well be clearin' out of this."

Constable Flynn was soon in sight again, returning in a succession of ducks and dives which indicated the proximity of some party whose observation was to be eluded. "Yes, he's comin' along," he said, "leastwise I'm sure it's himself—a low-sized black-lookin' feller, with legs a thought bandy, and a little brown ass." "Ay, that's Ody Rafferty," said the sergeant, "and an *ould lad*, I'm given to understand."

"But the quare part of it is," said Constable Flynn, "what way do you suppose he's got it done up? The jar's just cocked on the baste's back with a little dab of something about the size of your fist stuck a-top of it, by way of coverin' belike; but, bedad, it won't put us to much inconvanience searchin' the load. And he trampin' alongside lookin' as satisfied with himself as if he was deceivin' the nations around. The man must be a half-fool?"

"He might be after takin' a drop of it, and not be altogether himself," suggested Constable M'Kenna.

"There's ne'er a sign of it on him then. He's stompin' along as steady as a bench of judges."

"And he's got nobody else with him?"

"Divil the sign of a soul but himself."

"Would you like to know what the English of that is then?" said the sergeant, after brief reflection; "it's just a plant—a dodge they're up to, you may bet your boots it is. They've sent on the ould chap by himself to humbug us with the notion that he's the whole set of them; instead of which, to my sartin' knowledge there was to be at the least a couple more of them in this affair. And while we're took up discoursin' him, and arrestin' him, and at the heel of the hunt findin' very belike that he's got nothing in his ould jar but a sup of sour buttermilk or some such thrash—to be risin' the laugh on us—the others are schamin' to make off by some manner of route marchin' on this side or that of us, with the stuff we're lookin' for fixed up neat and tasty, may be in pottles of rushes by way of salmon—I've seen that sthratagem employed down about Lough Corrib—or goodness can tell what description of divilment, so as they'll be givin' us the slip. Sure it stands to reason 'tisn't for the want of a better contrivance they'd ever come foolin' down the road that fashion; they wouldn't ha' played such a tom-noddy trick except on a set purpose, you may depind."

"Troth, it's yourself has got the head on your shoulders, sergeant," said Constable Flynn.

"Then what are you thinkin' to do at all?" inquired Constable M'Kenna.

"Well, that must be partly accordin'. I'll step out and have a word with him as he comes by, and then if to my judgment it seems to be the way I'm supposin', faith, I'll just let him go along with himself. I'll not so far gratify him as to have him makin' a fool of me, and delayin' us from attendin' to the right boys. We mayn't have much chance of nabbin' them if they've took off at loose ends through the bog in this light, like so many wire-worm slitherin' in the crevices of a clod of clay. But we must scatter ourselves and do the best we can. Anyhow we'd get no satisfaction, only annoyance, out of dealin' with this ould concern that's comin' here."

When, therefore, Ody Rafferty and Jinny reached that point on the road, Sergeant Clarke had to be passed by, as he examined his boot-fastenings with a preoccupied air, and merely looked up to remark civilly: "It's a fine evenin'; gettin' a trifle duskish for travellin'.

By this time Ody can scarcely have been in his best form, intellectually speaking, as we may conclude from the fact that he pulled up and replied with a wink, which even through the dim twilight appeared egregious: " Ay, it's not too great an illumination we're gettin' whativer. But the divil dhrink up the hap'orth I've along wid me here that 'ud inthrist you for to be inspictin', sergeant; not if you'd the height of noonday to be doin' it by."

"Sure not at all," said the sergeant with polite deprecation, "why would you? But you're not distressin' the little ass any way with the size of the load you're puttin' on her."

"Begob no. It's long sorry I'd be to be givin' her any such thratement; nor yit to be disedifyin' her character, so to spake, wid lettin' her carry anythin' that's conthrary to regulations. So you perceive, sergeant, I can't offer you as much as a dhropeen to fill your flask, me hayro o' war, if you happen to have it about you."

"Ah, now's no time to be talkin' of drops," said the sergeant, to whom this overdone imbecility seemed exactly the snare into which he had set his face against falling, "I've got to go about my business. We're distribitin' poor-law notices. And so good evenin' to you."

Ody jogged on again, feeling confusedly that the interview had somehow been a failure. He had omitted to do or to say something that he had intended, but what he could not at all determine. And the thought bothered him so much, that when he had gone a mile or two further he sat down by the roadside to consider the point at leisure, while Jinny thriftily twitched herself up wispy mouthfuls of bent-grass from among the broom-clumps by the light of a drifting moon.

The police, for their part, continued to patrol, and look out, and lie dispersedly in ambush, according to the most approved methods, in the hope of surprising his accomplices, who of course were nowhere to be found. At length they gave it up, and began to return home, crestfallen, and rather disposed to regret that they had let their first and only take slip out of the meshes. Sergeant

Clarke had perhaps overreached himself by his crafty manœuvre. So when they presently came in sight of Jinny grazing beside her drowsy master, it seemed to them like a not to be expected repetition of an omitted opportunity, and even the sergeant felt that to again neglect it were now almost a tempting of Providence. Ody himself confirmed this impression. For roused by a stentorian cough from Constable M'Kenna, which affrighted the stillness further than a rifle-crack would have done at noon, he started up, and turned hurriedly to drive his beast off the road into the bog. He was three-parts asleep, and did so from mere force of habit; but Sergeant Clarke read in the action a consciousness of guilt, and at once gave the signal for pursuit. They had to skirt round a patch of swamp, and Ody, urging Jinny on with strange oaths and endearments, had covered some perilous ground before they overtook him. Flight and chase were alike hasty and ill-considered, and had an end natural enough when people blunder hot-foot through a wet bit of bog by the uncertain glimpses of a moon, who flickers out and in and out fitfully, like a defectively constructed revolving light. Ody Rafferty, and Jinny, and Sergeant Clarke, all tumbled headforemost over the edge of a deepish bog-hole.

If they had happened on one of those not rarely

occurring black crevasses, with smooth, ruthless-looking walls and a flooring of mirky glimmer which, after a few widening rings have melted away, will rest placid and unbetraying above whatever lies beneath, the chances are that they would still be there, testing the conservative properties of bog-water. The accident, however, was not so tragical. The hole into which Ody and his companions had fallen was a hollow of inartificial formation, with low broken banks at one end, where amid much splashing and bawling they were all brought to land A thorough drenching and a dazed recollection of some hideous struggling moments were the immediate consequences to the two men. But Jinny, having dislocated her neck, was quite dead.

This twofold shock restored Ody to his sober senses, though under the circumstances he could hit upon nothing more effectual to do with them than sit gloomily glowering at the limp brown body. Jinny was killed on him, and he had ignominiously delivered himself into the power of the enemy; the situation shattered even his self-confidence. Sergeant Clarke, on the other hand, was for the time being reduced to a state of aguish incapacity, so that the conduct of affairs devolved upon Constable M'Kenna.

" Be the powers of smoke, it seems to me we'd

all be the better of a taste of spirits, supposin' there was such a thing contiguous," he said, as he cut the strings which bound the whiskey-jar. Then he uncorked it and took a mouthful, intending to pass on the jar, but instead of doing so, he let it drop with a profane splutter and an agonised grimace. Both were in a measure excusable, for on a chill-breathing night, a wet and muddy man could scarcely imbibe a more comfortless draught than one composed of soapy water flavoured with sour goat's milk.

"What ould dish-washin's is it at all?" said Constable Flynn, watching the bluish-white stream gurgle out of the recumbent jar.

The sergeant was too shivery to point out the accuracy of his conjectures.

"The wife it must ha' been," said Ody, in a tone of concentrated bitterness, "she'll ha' been after doin' that on me while I was catchin' misfortnit Jinny there. She got the better of me, bedad. And the poor ass, that was the on'y sowl among the lot of us here wid a raisonable thought in her mind, must go for to be breakin' of her neck and drowndin' of herself dead. Och yis, the wife got greatly the better of me this time."

These two circumstances long remained a theme of galling and regretful memories to Ody Rafferty. I believe he was but slightly consoled by his own narrow escape from getting into trouble, or even by the fact that Sergeant Clarke, after being laid up for weeks with a bad rheumatic attack, exchanged to another station, and has not so far had an equally energetic successor at Duffclane. Mrs. Rafferty was dutiful enough to make profession in public of regret at Jinny's demise. But she said in confidence to a friend: "It's a loss on us, in coorse. Howsome'er there's no denyin' that Himself had one torminted wid the whillaballoo he made over her while she was to the fore. Sure, poor man, he's simple like, when he gits a foolish notion in his head."

I wish " Himself" could have heard her.

CHAPTER VI.

HERSELF.

IT is a dozen years or more since anybody, except some small wild bird or beast, has occupied the O'Driscolls' cabin, whose ruins may be traced beside the bit of road between the Kilfoyles' and Big Anne's, and it is much longer since one would have supposed it fit for even human habitation. But originally it was in some respects a better dwelling than any other in Lisconnel, being constructed of dense chinkless mud, instead of loosely cohering stones. For John O'Driscoll, who acted as his own architect and mason, could not abide the thoughts of any building material other than what he had been used to before he moved, on compulsion, northwards; and he gave himself no small additional labour in order to carry his point. Rushes for thatch he was fain to put up with; but he was certain that no people would ever get their health inside of them onnatural could stone walls; and the mud ones were undoubtedly warmer and more weather-tight. His neighbours, on the other hand, always maintained that the want of the preliminary clearance effected by the necessary collection for building purposes, was what caused his little bit of field to be so many degrees more infested with boulders than their own, which look hopeless enough, Heaven knows. But it is in reality a worse strip of ground; a mere skin of soil over the bleached limestone skeleton underneath, scarcely thicker than the sheet of paper on which the land-agent wrote his rent-receipt for the wistfully counted-out shillings and small grimy note. I do not wonder that this "holding" has never yet found another tenant; and so wholly obliterated are all signs of the O'Driscolls' long struggle against its sterile curse, that at the present day you might as reasonably regard it as a site for a stone-quarry as for a potato-plot.

A potato-plot it had to be, however, through many a toilsome season, though it adapted itself to this inappropriate end with so bad a grace that people, who are no strangers to phenomena of the kind, used yet to marvel how the O'Driscolls reared their children on it at all. Their own account of the matter was that they made a shift somehow, what with one thing and another; and I believe that both one thing and the other would, if analysed, have turned out to be chiefly Herself, as every one called Mrs. O'Driscoll, giving her the title which is commonly bestowed on the mistress of a household, but which is used with especial emphasis when she forms its main-spring and moving spirit.

She was a fair, buxom woman, of a physique not usual in Lisconnel, whose inhabitants are indeed very seldom fat and well-liking. The small children, it is true, are agreeably round and plump, but they roll out quickly once they grow to be any size, and are soon recognisable only by the dark-grey or violet-blue eyes, which have become melancholy instead of impish. In fact the young people of Lisconnel always make me think of Chaucer's poor scholar, who "lookede holwe, and therto soberly." The older people are not less lean, but as a rule somewhat cheerier of aspect, partly, perhaps, for just the reasons that make their juniors grave. So Herself, with her gracious curves and soft apple- and pear-blossom colouring, and rich golden-threaded brown hair, came upon you among her neighbours' Spanish-black tresses and slender, if not gaunt, forms, as something of a surprise. She would have made an ideal farmer's wife, on a farm of deeped-grassed green meadows and clover-scented pastures, where she might have queened it over curds and cream.

But she never had the management of a larger dairy than was supplied by the milk of a solitary goat; and her other possessions were in proportion. Certainly no woman could have made more of whatever property accrued to her; so perhaps it was only fair that she should be very poor, though as the aim of all her industry and contrivance was the welfare of other persons, it is on altruistic grounds justifiable to wish that she had been better off.

I do not know at what time of her life she passed a self-renouncing ordinance, but whenever it may have been, she was unaided by that apathetic placidity of temperament which makes it easy for some of us to renounce, if not ourselves, at any rate our nearest neighbours. She was full of energy and enterprise, and had the intuitive deftness of brain and hand which belongs almost exclusively to such women, enabling them to evolve their ingenious designs with as little visible effort and preparation as a flower shows in unfolding. This quality, by the way, is what has put into the heads of men, who can as a rule set about nothing without clumsy thinking processes, the delusion that they do all the world's inventing. The contrivances of Herself were manifold and wonderful, considering the resources at her command. Some of them were imitated by her neighbours, and will I dare say survive among their descendants when her name and story have long been forgotten. For instance, she once fashioned for her little daughter, who had a cut foot, a pair of shoes of plaited rushes, lined with the silky-flocked down of the bog-cotton, and carefully assorted feathers collected from the haunts of the hens. These turned out a great success, and at the present day you may now and then see a Lisconnel child with such foot-gear, probably not quite so dexterously shaped and put together, or so patiently renewed, as were little Molly O'Driscoll's. Of rushes, too, she wove the curious hanging-screens which for many a winter protected old Mrs. Kilfoyle from the worst of the draughts sighing through her profusely crannied walls; but the art of weaving them so thickly as to be impervious to almost any shrewd-breathing gust has died with Herself. And it was she who taught the children an elaborate game, still I believe peculiar to Lisconnel, preparations for which, consisting of small alternately black and white piles of peats and stones set arow with mysterous lines traced between, may be espied on smooth bits of ground along the road. Yet, after all, invention is not creation, and nothing short of that could have made the O'Driscolls' lot other than a hard one, in such barren places had their lines fallen. And at last Herself undertook a task which proved beyond her powers, and imagined a device which she was not able to perform.

When she first came to Lisconnel she was quite a young woman, and it is my belief that she would never have grown old if she could have kept her five children about her; but to do this would have been in itself almost as great a marvel as the discovery of an elixir of life. Of course the family broke up. Michael, the eldest son, enlisted, and only came home once just before his regiment sailed for the Cape. His blue and gold were beautiful to look upon, and set the children marching to and fro for weeks after with a tin-can drum. When they came towards his mother's door, she bribed them with hoarsely-creaking whistles, which she had a knack of making out of hollow hemlock stalks, to go away with their martial music in the opposite direction. And not long afterwards the elder of the two girls got married. However, she did not go to any formidable distance, and there were still Jack and Terence and Rose left at home.

Then began a series of bad seasons, in the course of which the married daughter emigrated with her husband, and wrote home word—as well as one could make out by means of conjectural emendations—that "the States was not too quare to live in, and they all had their healths finely, glory be to God." After that letter, the States, and the possibility of resorting thither, were much talked of under the O'Driscolls' roof. At first Herself joined in the discussions with a sparkle in her eyes; for she was not in years more than middle-aged, and in heart and hope younger, perhaps, than any of them. Leaving the old country would, no doubt, be very sad, and crossing the ocean rather terrible, but they would all be together, and it was miserable work to see the children looking so starved and perished. Molly, too, would be there to meet them —"the States" as mapped out in the O'Driscolls' minds were about the size of the Town down beyant, where you could scarcely miss any one you were looking out for, if you streeled around a bit—and who could tell but that Mick might be there or thereabouts? It stood to reason that they could not be very far asunder, when they were both in foreign parts. Herself began to weave plans as busily as a linnet weaves its nest in the spring, and her thoughts went out into the future as undauntedly as a swallow starts on a migration.

But one day her husband spoke half a dozen words which suddenly stopped all her hoping and planning, as a small bird's flight is stopped by the blow of a stone. He said something which showed that he had no intention of leaving Lisconnel, and that he nevertheless assumed the children would go. This sentence was the result of a sharp engagement between his conscience and his wishes—doubtfully the battle stood. Complete victory for his conscience would have been agreement to go; for his wishes, a denunciation of the whole project in strong terms which he knew would ensure its abandonment. So he only attained to a compromise, and even that had been dearly won. John O'Driscoll was many years older than his wife, and hard work and harder fare—what there was of it—had aged his tall, gaunt frame before its time. Perhaps he knew instinctively that he could not bear transplantation; but at any rate he knew without need of instinct what days of desolation he was refusing to avert from himself, when he said, " And ye'd write to us here?" the words which so filled Herself with dismay.

For a little while she could resolutely take it for granted that the plan would just be given up; but as the talk went on, and she perceived that this was not the case, she froze into mute despair, where she sat listening at the open doorway in the chill December breath which brought her light enough to mend Jack's coat. Her husband, conscious of his significant speech, did not overlook its effect upon her, and presently, when the others had gone out, he said, in a half deprecatory way: " The lads do be tired of starvin'—the crathurs."

But she only nodded her head faintly, looking straight before her, and could make no other answer.

After a few days, however—few be all such evil days—she began again to take part in the discussions. And it now seemed that her interest had fully revived, and she could plan and scheme as eagerly as ever, though the sparkle had gone out of her eyes. She said never a word to discourage or deter the lads. On the contrary, she actually incited and persuaded Rose, who at first declared vehemently that she could not possibly go and leave them all alone. Her mother knew that the girl was restless and wearying for a turn in the bleak road of her joyless days. So she said that she would be aisier in her mind if she knew that the lads had their sister along with them, and that it would be a sin to throw away so good a chance for them all to go together happy and contint; and that she and the father would be fine company for one another, and would be kep' heartened up hearin' from them now and agin—and maybe they'd come home to her one of those days.

The poor children protested that they would be writing home continual, ay, and sending over the money for the rint; if it wasn't on'y for the sake of helping that a-way, sorra the thing else would take them out of the ould place. But suppose now the pitaties took and failed agin this summer, how would she and father git on at all? Not that they themselves could do a hand's turn if they sted, except to be aiting all before them. There was the turf-cutting, to be sure, could father conthrive that left to himself? Ah, maybe they'd a right to give up the notion, and thry gitting along the way they were.

Herself felt in every fibre that this would be as the return of a golden age. But she said sure not at all. She had her goat, and her hens, and the young pig, and no fear but they'd do right well. And when once the fine weather had come—she was looking out as she spoke over a frost-bound bog, with powdery white drifts like ashes in its black creases, and the keening wind smelt of the coming snow—why the time would slip away plisant enough. No doubt it was the contemplation of those pleasant times that made such broad silvery streaks in her brown hair before the swift-footed day of parting arrived.

The children went on an afternoon in the early spring, when the evenings are light and cold. Jack had made jokes about different things all the morning, and his mother had laughed at them, which was a more or less equal division of labour. But for the last hour or so he could think of only two. One was: "Sure we'll be in the way of gettin grand say-fishin' now entirely;" and the other: "Bedad, I think we'd a right to take ould Fanny (the goat) thravellin' wid us too." This last jest occurred to him when he saw his mother milking the creature that Rose might have a bottleful to take with her for a drink. He was reduced to repeating them alternately; however, they served the purpose just as well as a greater variety would have done. His father went out and gathered stones in the worst corner of the field. He was not quite sure whether he were glad or sorry to find how heavy the middling-sized ones seemed to lift. Sometimes he said to himself: "I'd ha' been a burthen on them if I'd ha' went;" and sometimes, "I shouldn't maybe ha' kep' her back." The others made no pretences in particular.

Herself watched them out of sight over the brow of the low hill. All the while she was thinking how one of them might at the last moment fling down his bundle, and declare with forcible asseverations that he would not go a fut, as the Cullinanes' son had done not so long before, which would, of course, have been a great pity. Somehow she thought Jack would be the most likely to do that, he was a foolish, poor lad. But, alas, the three figures walked on and on till the ridge hid them; they had not even forgotten anything that they could run back to fetch. Then she went back into the house and spoke cheerfully to her husband, who sat huddled up by the fire, while she put away the cold potatoes left over from dinner which nobody had eaten. He did not answer her for a long time, and then only said, " Whisht, honey, whisht." However, in the course of the evening they said, between the two of them, nine times that the childer had a fine day for startin', any way, and seven times that they might be hearing from them next month, *early*. They may have said nothing else, but that was in itself a fair allowance of conversation.

After this black day had passed, it was several years before any very noticeable incident occurred in the history of Herself and her husband. It may be epitomised in the statement that they got along pretty middling. Now and again a curious little scrawl came from overseas for them, with a money-order in it sometimes—always when the young people had been able to scrape together anything worth sending ; but dollars are scarce occasionally, even in the States, and as Terence wrote, " the dareness of some things was intense." John O'Driscoll worked harder than before at his potatoes and turf, now that he had no sons to help him, but Herself grew sadly out of her industrious habits. She who was once rarely to be seen without a bit of knitting, or plaiting, or patching in progress, who would pick bunches of ox-eye daisies and poppies to fill the house's window-pane with, rather than remain idle, or fashion quaint ornaments for her dresser of various flaggers and horsetails and bulrushes, and such other bog growths, would now often sit for half an hour at a time with her hands empty before her. All the purposes of her life seemed to be flapping aimlessly about her, as a sail does when the fair wind drops or veers. I fear she cannot have had the true artist's spirit, since, failing an audience to be pleased and applaud, she ceased to take any intrinsic pleasure in her productions. She hadn't the heart, she said herself, to be mindin' about such whim-whams. And now, of course, she had no longer any one to criticise and admire except her husband, who had not by nature any appreciation for things of the kind, though to gratify her he would look mournfully at what she showed him, and say that it was a great little affair, or that she was a terrible woman for consthructions. But she was to lose even this encouragement.

One rainy autumn John O'Driscoll fell ill, and after moping about for a few days, took to his bed, which was composed of mud and rushes, drier, it is true, than the same materials as they existed outside his door. Herself nursed him desperately, and dared not fear that it was anything serious, until one night he began saying " Wo, Sheila," and

"Hup, Blossom," to the horses he had ploughed with in his younger days, and twisted his arms as if he were turning the plough-handle at a difficult corner. And then despair stabbed her with an icy thrust.

Two or three evenings before that, old Mick Ryan, who in those days was still able-bodied and active, handed a little dark object to his daughter Biddy, and bade her run over with it to John O'Driscoll. It was a very small morsel of the tobacco, which Mick treasured so fondly that he could not fill his pipe without some effort; whence we may calculate with how much he gave any away.

"I question is he able for smokin'," said Biddy, looking doubtfully at the fragment. "Maryanne said he seemed uncommon bad when she was in there this mornin', and Herself told her he hadn't took bite or sup, you might say, these two days back."

"A good pipe of 'baccy's better nor mate and dhrink to a man any day, well or ill," said Mick; "run along and be bringin' it to him."

Biddy had run obediently some way, when her father called her back again: "You might as well be takin' that too," he said, giving her another little lump which he had in the meanwhile forced himself to cut off. It represented, however, more than his whole day's allowance.

On the morning after John O'Driscoll's mind had begun to wander, Biddy Ryan came to the O'Driscolls' door. Herself had seen her coming, and met her on the threshold with a little wisp of something rolled up in paper. "It's your father's bit of tobaccy, Biddy," she said, "that was never touched, and I put it aside for him, thinkin' he might have a use for it, and thank him kindly all the same."

"Oh dear, you do look tired and bad this day, Mrs. O'Driscoll," said Biddy, "and what way's Himself at all?"

"He's gone," said his wife; "he's gone since afore it was light this mornin'. The fever he had on him went then, and all the strenth seemed to die out of him. And he's gone."

Biddy began to cry. "Och, Mrs. O'Driscoll, darlint," she said, "may the saints above pity you this day. Ochone, but it's desolit you're left, woman dear, rael desolit."

"Ay, I am so," Herself said, assenting in an indifferent, preoccupied way, as if to an uninteresting proposition about some other person.

Perhaps at no moment did she fully emerge from this half-stunned state. The neighbours generally say that she was never the same woman again, which is true enough—never herself again, even in name, for they now spoke of her as the

Widdy O'Driscoll. And old Mrs. Kilfoyle said she thought the crathur had in a manner given herself up; but this was not exactly the case. She had still a purpose in life to which she passionately clung. When she had sold her pig, and her goat, and all her chickens, in order that John's coffin might not be supplied from the House, she set herself to the task of keeping the soul in her body, and the roof over her head, until the childer returned. But she now no longer seemed to anticipate that event as a keen personal joy for herself; she was considering it in their interest, and from their point of view. They would be so cruelly disappointed if they came home and found nobody left. "We done wrong," she said, "to let them go. Sure, what's to become of them, if they landed back into the middle of disolation, and they thinkin' to find me sittin' be the bit o' fire, or maybe takin' a look out of the door? For who'd there be to send them word I was quit? Wirrasthrew, it's lost altogether and miserable they'd be, Heaven purtect them. But sure, I'll do me endeavours to bide and keep goin' till then, plase God."

In those days Mrs. O'Driscoll would have looked a melancholy figure even to strangers who did not remember her in her earlier comeliness. For when six months do the work of a dozen years, they accomplish their task roughly, and with no relenting touches. She had shrunk and withered in form and face. " Eh, woman dear," Mrs. Sheridan once said to her, " I'm thinkin' that ould gown of yours has in a manner outgrown you." The soft bloom on her cheeks had dwindled into hard little streaks among many-meshed fine lines, and she walked with bent shoulders, and the uncertain step of an old woman who has not any definite goal in view. All this did not surprise her neighbours, because, though they were unaware how her dwelling, still unchanged in outward aspect, had become the lair of a fearful thing, which needed to be approached with strange and piteous precautions lest it should leap forth and rend her, they yet felt that the forlornness of her plight would well account for these sad outward signs of alteration. But there was one thing about her which puzzled them. They could not see any reason why she should have grown so fond of colloguing with Mad Bell. That this was the case nobody could doubt, for as often as she went past the door of Big Anne and her co-tenants to fill a bucket at the pool, she invariably now stopped on her way home at the angle of the flat-topped dyke along by their field, which used to be Mad Bell's favourite roosting-place, and if she were not visible, would generally loiter about there until she appeared. It is true that Mad Bell, who was capricious in her attachments, had in this instance gone with the multitude so far as to entertain a decided regard for Mrs. O'Driscoll, and would pause in the midst of the most impassioned song to nod and grin at her. Their intercourse, however, had not been wont to go much further, since Mad Bell, except when at fitful intervals "the humour took her for talkin'," was a silent and unexpansive person. But now Mrs. O'Driscoll might be seen by the half-hour together sitting on the dyke beside the little wizened yellow-visaged figure, and "gabbin' away as thick as thieves;" and that too, mind you, on a day when she'd as like as not pass a sensible body on the road, and scarce seem to take notice. The neighbours' perplexity had a tinge of grievance in it.

One day it chanced that the pair had an interview a bit out on the bog, near the place where Brian Kilfoyle and his wife were cutting long-tufted grass under a bank for their pig. Mrs. O'Driscoll had espied the gleam of Mad Bell's red petticoat against the black peat, and had sped after it rather than return home unfortified by a word with its wearer. As the Kilfoyles moved along the bank, twitching up bunches of the tangled green blades, they gradually came closer to the two women who were sitting on the other side, and when Mrs. Brian arrived within earshot of their discourse, Mrs. O'Driscoll was just saying: "So, as I said, Mad Bell, I ought to be steppin' back to git the water on the fire, in case by any odd chance Himself happint home to-night; not that it's anyways likely, for he's after gittin' a long job down below at Hilfirthy's—thinnin' mangolds and weedin' turnips they are. I wouldn't wonder meself if he wasn't home a fut before the end of the week."

"Yis they will, och they will, and they'll think him a gintleman borrn, they will," Mad Bell murmured absently. It was the refrain of a favourite ditty, but did not throw much light upon the matter in hand.

"And the lads are along wid him," Mrs. O'Driscoll continued, "and I tould you Rose was gone to stay a couple of days wid her sister away at Lisnadrum. It makes the house seem lonesome like, Mad Bell, me dear; howsome'er, it's just for a while you know. It's not as if I hadn't their comin' back to look to."

Mad Bell only nodded curtly and went on humming; but it was precisely this passive acquiescence which made her a valuable confidante to Mrs. O'Driscoll, who continued, not discouraged: "I'm thinkin' after all 'twill be scarce worth me while to be puttin' down any more pitaties this evenin' on the chanst of their comin'. The could ones I have over from this mornin' 'll do grandly for me, if I warm them up; and even so, there might be a few left to crisp for the lads in case they were home agin breakfast-time to-morra. Jack does have an oncommon fancy for a crisp pitaty; he always had iver since his two hands were the size to be houldin' one. So good-night to you kindly, Mad Bell. I'll have a sup of water boilin', and then if they do come——"

At this moment Mrs. Brian accidentally pulled a clattering stone down along with her wisp of grass and Mrs. O'Driscoll, startled, saw that she had been speaking to more ears than Mad Bell's. She looked confused and disconcerted by the discovery, and said in an apologetic tone: "Ah, Mrs. Brian, sure I was just in a manner romancin', if you happint to notice. 'Deed it's foolish enough, very belike, but she doesn't mind, and the truth is, the bit of a house there does be that quite and lonesome on me these times and I comin' in, that I'm afeard, troth it's afeard I am goin' back to it, onless I've somethin' made up in me mind to hould off the thought like. For, goodness help me, when I'm steppin' up to the door, if I was to be thinkin' all the while 'twould be that same way, wid niver the sound of a voice or the stir of a fut inside for iver and ivermore—sure I'd be fit to go disthracted outright, so

I would. Och, but it's that I go in dread of. And there's the raison why I keep lettin' on they're on'y away tempor'y. In coorse I know it's makin' a fool of meself I am, but it's a sort o' comfort all the same. And it seems more nathural when I get tellin' it, and talkin' about them to somebody else. *She* niver throubles herself, the crathur, whativer you let on to her, or minds to be conthradictin'. Sure now, there's no sin in it, is there, ma'am? when it's on'y yourself you're deceivin'. So I just pluther away to her for me own contintmint."

"And bedad I hadn't the heart," Mrs. Brian said, when relating the incident to her friends, "for to say anythin' agin it to her; though it's a quare kind of consowlment it seems to me. But och, she must be hard put to it these times to find any at all."

"If she'd say an odd prayer for them now and agin," said the widow M'Gurk with some sternness, "she'd be better employed, and there might be more sinse in it than conthrivin' ould invintions."

"She might, to be sure," Mrs. Brian said, doubtfully, "but accordin' to me own experience there's nought aisier than to be sayin' one's prayers and thinkin' of diffrint things at the same time, and that's no disthraction aither to a body's mind. You might as well be sthrivin' to keep the win' out wid a sieve full of holes."

"I do suppose there's some things there's no use tryin' to contind wid, and that's a fac'," said old Mrs. Kilfoyle, "if one could make one's mind up to believe it. But maybe, plase God, she won't be spared over long."

Mrs. O'Driscoll, however, stuck persistently to her forlorn device. Even on days when Mad Bell was not forthcoming to act as interlocutor, she would pause at the accustomed point on her way home, and her lips might be seen moving, as if she were romancing to herself. Once Pat Ryan, who passed her by on an occasion when she had been bringing in a load of turf, reported a new phase of self-delusion. "For," said he, "I give you me word, she'd her creel there set down on the dyke, and first she'd take one little bit of a sod, and lay it on the flat of the stone, and 'That's Roseen's' she'd say, and then she'd put another beside it, and sez she: 'and that's what I got the lads—and here's for Molly,' sez she, and so on. Then she'd be puttin' them back in the creel, but she'd stop to take another look at them, makin' as if she was considherin', and 'Maybe,' sez she, 'this here 'ud do better for the boys, and Molly might liefer have the pink-coloured one.' That's the way she kep' talkin' to herself, and I couldn't think what she was at, till the idee came into me head 'twas lettin' on she was to be comin' home from the Town, wid thrifles of presents in her basket for the childher— and they grown and gone. But all the while you could perceive she knew right well she was just persuadin' herself agin her raison ; on'y she couldn't abide to be thinkin' so. Sure, 'twas melancholious," said Pat, "to see her there on the roadside in the rain, fiddlin' about with them ould scraps of turf-sods, all be herself."

When the neighbours heard it, many of them shook their heads oracularly, and said 'twouldn't be apt to go on that-a way for very long. But how long it might have gone on in the natural course of things cannot now be known, for it was brought to an end by the interposition of the law's strong arm. It was not, I am sure, " the childer's " fault that for some time before their father's death their scrawls and money-orders had arrived but seldom at Lisconnel. The contents of the communications which did get there showed plainly that they were themselves struggling along painfully enough in the new world, and likewise that several other scrawls had failed to reach their destination—not a surprising result, when one considers their quaintly enigmatical superscriptions—and may at the present writing be stowed unavailingly away in blind or dead-letter departments. But this falling off of remittances, conjoined with a series of bad seasons, hastened the accumulation of the

O'Driscolls' arrears; and when John died, the land-agent wrote to his employer at the Carlton that the widow's ever paying up appeared to be an utterly hopeless matter—which was quite true. Her neighbours were indeed ready to lend her, as far as possible, a helping hand, but it could not extend itself to the payment of her rent, and to grub that out of her screed of stony ground was a task beyond her powers. The land-agent also wrote that the poor woman, who seemed to be an uncivilised, feeble-minded sort of creature, would be much better in the Union, and that as she must at any rate be got rid of, he had taken immediate steps for serving her with the necessary notices. The woman's own view of the case was in sum: "Sure, what would become of the childer if she would be put out of it?" an argument the futility of which it would have been hard to make her understand.

She was put out of it, however, one blustery autumn day, when the sub-sheriff's party and the police had caused an unwonted stir and bustle all the morning on the Duffclane road, along which so many feet seldom pass in a twelvemonth. The district was reported disturbed, and therefore a squadron of dragoons had been brought from the nearest garrison, a tedious way off, to protect and overawe. Their scarlet tunics and brass helmets enlivened the outward aspect of the proceedings vastly, making such a gorgeous pageant as our black bogland has perhaps never witnessed before or since. Not a gossoon but worshipped the stately horses as they passed, and thought their plumed and burnished riders almost as supernaturally superb. But it must be owned that the latter were for the most part in very human bad-tempers. In fact when they ascertained the nature and scope of the duty on which they had come so far, some of them said a choleric word with such emphasis that their superiors were obliged to choose between deafness and mutiny, or at least insubordination, and discreetly preferred the lesser evil.

When the invading force entered Lisconnel, which it did among afternoon beams, just begun to mellow and slant dazzlingly, it found an ally in old Mrs. Kilfoyle, inasmuch as she enticed Mrs. O'Driscoll to pay her a visit at the critical moment of its arrival. The old woman had recognised the widow O'Driscoll's fate as one of those things with which there is no contending, and had said to herself and her daughter-in-law: "Where's the use of havin' them risin' a row there wid draggin' her out, the crathur, God pity her, that 'll niver quit, for sartin, of her own free will? I'll just step over to her and axe her to come give me a hand wid mendin' the bottom that's fallin' out of th'ould turf-creel. She did always be great at them jobs, and always ready to do a body a good turn, I'll say that for her."

"'Deed yis," said Mrs. Brian.

So it came about that at the time when the forcible entrance of her cabin was being effected, Mrs. O'Driscoll was out of sight in the Kilfoyles' dark little room, where the two Mrs. Kilfoyles detained her as long as they could. But in the end they were not able to prevent the evicted tenant from joining the group of angry and scared and woe-begone faces, gathered as near the doomed dwelling as the authorities would permit, and from saying, " Wirra, wirra," in a half-bewildered horror, as she saw each one more of her few goods and chattels added to the little heap of chaos into which her domestic world had changed fast by her door. It was decreed that her cabin should be not only unroofed but demolished, because, as an old bailiff dolefully remarked, " There niver was any tellin' where you'd have those boyos. As like as not they'd land the thatch on to it agin, the first minnit your back was turned, as aisy as you'd clap your ould caubeen on your head, and there'd be the whole botheration over agin as fresh as a daisy." Therefore when the ancient, smoke-steeped, weather-worn covering had been plucked from off the skeleton rafters, and lay strewn around in flocks and wisps like the wreck of an ogre's brown wig, the picks and crowbars came into play, for it was before the days of battering-ram or maiden. The mud walls were solid and thick, yet had to yield, and presently a broad bit of the back wall fell outward all of a piece, as no other sort of masonry falls, with a dull, heavy thud like a dead body. The limewashed inner surface, thus turned up skywards, gleamed sharply, despite all its smoke-grime, against the drab clay, and though the interior had been very thoroughly dismantled, a few small pictures were still visible, nailed on the white. As the cordon of police and other officials fell back a pace or so to avoid the toppling wall, the widow M'Gurk seized the opportunity to make a sally and capture one of these derelict ornaments. It was a Holy Family, a crudely coloured print, all crimson and blue, with a deep gilt border, such as you might purchase for a halfpenny any day.

"Ay, sure it's great men you are intirely to be evictin' the likes of them," she cried shrilly, waving her loot aloft, as she was hustled back to a respectful distance, and Lisconnel responded with a low and sullen murmur.

But Mrs. O'Driscoll's attention was very opportunely taken up by the restoration of this piece of property. "Och, woman alive," she said, "and it was Himself brought me that one—give it to me into me hand. Sure I remimber the day yit, as if the sun hadn't gone down on it. Th'ould higgler Finny had come up wid his basket, and while some of the rest did be about gittin' a few trifles, I was in an oncommon admiration of this; howsome'er I hadn't a pinny to me name to be spindin' on anythin' in the world, so I let him go. But sure Himself met him below on the road, and happint to have a ha'pinny about him, and so he brought it home to me. I mind I run out and borried a tack from poor Mick Ryan to put it up wid. Ah dear, look now at the tear it's got at the top comin' off."

This damage seemed for the time being to concern her more than any of her other troubles, and she allowed herself to be drawn away on the pretext of depositing the picture safely in the Kilfoyles' cabin, where she remained until the invaders had departed from Lisconnel. Everybody else watched them trooping off over the bogland, with brass and scarlet flashing and glowing splendidly in windy gleams of the sunset. They had gone a long way before the purple-shadowed gloaming had swallowed up the last far-espied glitter.

With the Kilfoyles she found a lodging for some time, but she ended her days at the widow M'Gurk's, where there was no less hospitality and more spare room. She was persuaded to make the move chiefly by the consideration that she would there be nearer the crest of the hill. For the dominant dread which now brooded over her life—we so seldom fall too low for special fear—was the home-coming of the childer: "And they to be steppin' along, the crathurs, expectin' no harm, and then when they're up the hill, and in sight of our bit of a house, all of a suddint to see there was no thrace of it on'y a disolit roon. They might better keep the breadth of the ocean-say between them and that." She seemed to be continually living through in imagination this terrible moment, and grew more and more eager to avert it. "If I could get e'er a chanst to see them comin' the road," she said, "and give them warnin' afore they'd crossed the knockawn, 'twouldn't come so crool hard on them." And with that end in view, she spent many an hour of the bleak winter days which followed her eviction in looking out from the unsheltered hillside towards Duffclane. It was vain now for any neighbour to profess a firm belief that they would never return, just as confidently as he or she had formerly been used to predict their appearance one of these days. Mrs. O'Driscoll listened meekly while it was pointed out to her how probably they had settled themselves down over there for good and all, and got married maybe; or who could tell that one of them mightn't have been took bad, and have gone beyond this world altogether the same as his poor father? But then she went and looked out again. The young Doynes and Sheridans, who at that time were quite small children, remember how she would stop them when she met them, and bid them be sure, if ever by any chance they saw Rose or one of the lads coming along, to mind and tell them that their father was gone, and she was put out of it, but that Mrs. M'Gurk was givin' her shelter, and no fear they wouldn't find her; and to bid them make haste, all the haste they could.

It must have been when she was on the watch one perishing March day that she caught the cold which carried her off with very little resistance on her part. She was herself too weak, and still too much taken up with the childer's affairs, to fret about the fact that the expenses of her "buryin'" would certainly be defrayed by the House, but it distressed Lisconnel seriously, and would never have been permitted to occur, could the requisite sum have been by any means amassed. The circumstance added some gloom to the sorrowful mood in which her neighbours saw another procession pass over the hill on a still wet morning, when the rain rustled all along the road, and the grey mist curtains were closely drawn.

None of the childer have come back again, and it may now be hoped that they never will.

CHAPTER VII.

THUNDER IN THE AIR.

CONSIDERING everything, Lisconnel musters as large a congregation as could be expected for Mass down beyant on Sundays and saints' days. But then so many things have to be considered, including primarily those long miles of desolate road, that its numbers are actually small. For when from the population of the place you have deducted the people who are too young, or too old, or crippled like Peter and Peg Sheridan, or minding babies and invalids; and from the residuum again abstract the men who prefer basking in the sun, should it happen to spread that poor man's feast, and the boys who under any meteorological conditions whatever would choose rather to rush and yell about the wild bog than sit still within four solemn walls, you will find no very imposing contingent left. Of course there are many days of the year when wind and weather permit nobody to attempt the journey. But a few people perform it with much regularity; the widow M'Gurk, for instance, a strong and quick walker, and Big Anne, who stumps on steadily and perseveringly, and says, " Musha, good gracious, glory be to God, it's here I am," when she arrives. Little old Mrs. Kilfoyle, too, might for many years be met pattering along with a clean white flannel petticoat over her head, and her face looking out quaintly through the pocket-hole. This is the fashionable substitute for a cloak in Lisconnel, and Mrs. Kilfoyle's venerable blue-cloth hooded garment, soon after it came into her possession by inheritance, had been stolen by a passing vagrant, to the lasting impoverishment of her family in the female line. She used to trot on with a briskness and staying power which did her son Brian's heart good to see. When the neighbours commented upon it, and said sure, bedad, she was as young as any of them, he was as much pleased as if some one had guaranteed him ten years' good harvests. For by that time she must have been verging upon eighty, according to conjecture—in Lisconnel our ages are always more or less matters of guess-work, once they begin to be reckoned by years. But one Sunday—it was a mild, mellow-lighted September afternoon—she grew so very tired on the way back, that they had the work of the world getting her home, and she never went to Mass again; though, by one of those fictions which make life endurable, it was always understood that she would resume the practice when the weather did be something drier, or warmer, or cooler, please goodness, coming on Easter or Michaelmas. And Brian found this a sadly shrunken source of satisfaction.

During the late summer and early autumn, Lisconnel is most frequently and numerously represented in the little chapel near the Town, partly, perhaps, because its inhabitants are at this season better fed, and have consequently more energies to spare for extra exertions, and partly because in the pleasant breezy blue and white mornings mothers and wives and sisters find it easier to beat up recruits for their three-hours' trudge to first Mass. Even on rare occasions when there is a station held at Duffclane, which cuts a couple of miles off their tramp, the start has to be a timely one, made while your long shadow eclipses many twinkling stars in the grass as it slides before you, and while the air is still fresh with dew. On such mornings as these, quite a procession sometimes goes over the knockawn, the white cloaks and the shirtsleeves gleaming with a stainlessness and snowiness which always puzzles me, when I look into the dark doors whence they issue.

I do not think that Lisconnel afflicts itself much about its remoteness from chapel, and this equanimity is in a measure due to the attitude adopted by old Father Rooney, who has for over forty years been its parish priest. In his most active days he recognised how impossible it would be to establish any very close connections between himself and that furthest outlying shred of his widely scattered cure, and a natural benevolence of disposition inclined him to console his parishioners for their inevitable stinting in the matter of his ministrations. Perhaps, also, the breadth of the spacious physical horizon which he had before his eyes as he rode about the bogs, may have somehow influenced his mental vision.

"Me good woman," he exhorted Mrs. M'Gurk one day, when she had been lamenting the probability that it might be her husband's fate to die without his clergy, "you should not be making your mind too uneasy on that score. Send for me of course, and if by any means I can come up to you, well and good. But if I'm prevented, you've no call to be supposing that you'll be left without every sort of assistance for that reason. Likely enough I may be all the while riding off Sallinmore ways or Drumesk ways as fast as I can contrive, but I'm not taking the blessed saints and the Mother of Mercy, and the rest following along with me same as if I was, so to speak, showing them their road. They know where they're wanted as well as you or I, you may depend, and won't be asking either of our leaves to get there." Mrs. M'Gurk was slightly shocked and greatly relieved by this view of the matter. I am not prepared to deny that if her circumstances had been less utterly poverty-stricken, Father Rooney might have sincerely believed it his duty to point out a more expensive method of quieting her misgivings. But extreme indigence has some immunities, and these people of Lisconnel are such empty-handed travellers between life and death that no one can be much tempted to demand this kind of toll from them on the way.

Father Carroll, who sometimes assists Father Rooney, takes a rather sterner view of things, which, however, does not count for much here or there, owing to his smaller popularity. The people generally speak of him as "the cross priest," less because they really know anything to the disadvantage of his temper, than because his harsh-featured, blue-shaven face looks somewhat grim beside the other's kindly ruddy countenance and fringe of white hair. To some persons Father Carroll's outward man would suggest a suspicion that he was habitually guarding dark secrets; but I do not believe that this is the case. He is on more substantial grounds considered to have "a great eye entirely for a good horse."

One Saint Peter's Day he came up to Lisconnel on an urgent sick call, and when departing fell in with Terence Doyne, a wildish lad, to whom he put the question why he had not gone to Mass that morning with his parents, instead of fishing for pinkeens along by the river, appending as a sort of corollary—which, we know, is often more puzzling than the original proposition—a request to be informed what effect on his final destinies Terence anticipated from such a line of conduct. Terence replied : " Whethen, your Riverince, I'll be right enough I'm thinkin', Mass or no Mass, wid me mother down below there prayin' away for me like iverything you could name. Sure you wouldn't say they'd go for to be makin' a fool of her, lettin' her waste her time axin' for nothin' she'll git. If they would, she might as well ha' been after thim pinkeens, that's as slithery to try catch as little ould divils. Did your Riverince iver hare tell there was troutses in the bit of sthrame along yonder?"

Terence was trying to slip away from the point, but Father Carroll would not be evaded, and said : " No, Terence ; to be certain your mother will experience the benefit of her prayers. But suppose she's granted something else better, instead of the saving of a young slieveen like yourself—and such a thing is easy enough to imagine—where'd you be then, me fine lad?"

This presentment of the case somewhat flabbergasted Terence, and his Reverence would probably have had the last word, if Terence's brother Matt, a smaller and more reflective gossoon, had not intervened, saying confidently: "There's nary no such a thing to be had. Sorra another thing 'ud pacify me mother, if anything went agin him—not if it was the iligintest could be consaived. She's always had such a wish for him"—Matt pointed to Terence—"as niver was. Musha, but it's a fine time them saints would be havin'; it's pluther, pluther, pluther, she'd go, like th'ould hummin'-machine they had threshin' oats down at Hilfirthy's below, and divil a minnit's paice 'ud one of thim git wid her, if anybody looked crooked at him."

Father Carroll had not an argument ready, so he only said, "The poor woman seems likely to have her own work with the pair of you," and the advantage may be considered to have rested with the brothers.

Several years after this, a most brilliant July Sunday rose upon Lisconnel, and by seven o'clock the people bound for chapel were prepared to start. It was a hot, very still morning. The invisible hand, which is almost always combing the rushes and sedges about the marshy pools, had for once left them to stand straight, and there was not a breath stirring that could have carried the lightest cloud-fleck across the deep speedwell-blue of the sky, where, however no clouds were to be seen. Yet old Mick Ryan, who was sunning himself at his door, said that the weather looked none too fine, and wouldn't hold up much longer. "It's too clare altogether over yonder," he said, pointing to the far-off horizon, against which a sharp peak was delicately outlined in faint wild-violet colour. "We'll be apt to be havin' a crack of thunder prisently; it's in the air." But the others said they saw no signs of it; and it would be a quare thing to have thunder so early in the month.

When the chapel-bound party had gone a little way beyond the hill, they met Terence Doyne coming from the opposite direction. "Is it home you're goin', Terence?" said his sister Stacey. "I'm glad of that now, for you'll be company to mother, and Matt's away off somewheres down the bog." For Mrs. Doyne was ailing, and Stacey had been divided between a particularly strong wish to attend Mass this morning, and a feeling that she ought to stay and keep her mother heartened up. She now walked on with a salved conscience, though, judging by Terence's appearance, one might have thought him likely to prove rather a wearing companion, his look being as of one who has a grievance and resents it. And, as a matter of fact, his mother, so far from being cheered up when some time afterwards he stooped in at her doorway, felt her heart gripped again by a temporarily staved-off dread. She had supposed him safely on his way to Mass.

Since he had come back, however, she earnestly desired him to remain indoors, and she made conversation perseveringly under the discouragement of brief and grumpy replies. She hoped she was talking him into good-humour, until he suddenly glanced round the shadow-hung walls and said: "There's one of the loys took. Where's Matt?"

"Och, away outside maybe — just trapesin' about," said Mrs. Doyne with a start. "And so I was tellin' you, Judy Ryan sez to me they were half through——"

"That chap's as solid as a gob of mud when he's took a notion in his fool's head," Terence went on disregardfully; "I know what he's after—cuttin' sods in the bank where I've tould him times and agin there isn't a spade-load of good slane turf, let alone it's bein' twyst as far to carry as from the place I was showin' them yesterday." He turned towards the door, but his mother, whose head and hands had begun to tremble, said piteously: "Sure niver mind about it this instiant, Terence avic; where's the hurry? What were we sayin' about the Ryans? It was somethin' divartin' enough, I know, on'y it's just passed out of me head, till I remimber it in another minnit—wait now—Terence honey, would you fancy a bit of the griddle-cake Mrs. Kilfoyle brought me? There was a good bit over that I couldn't ait last night, and I put it away on purpose for you to be havin' it. Beautiful wholemale it is, she was sint a presint of." Our mothers never quite believe that we have fully outgrown the lure of sugared bread-and-butter, or the like; and perhaps they hold a not altogether ungrounded faith. Then as Terence was striding on gracelessly past this offer, she said: "Och then, stay a bit wid me, jewel; sure it's lonesome I do be, and Stacey away all the mornin', and niver a sowl for me to pass a word wid. And me head's bad. Sure you might stop in a while when I ax you."

She so seldom made a point-blank appeal for anything on her own behalf, that Terence was impressed, and sat down, to her great relief, upon the ledge of the dresser, which jingled all its jugs and cups every time he swung his legs. Furthermore he said, "Y'ould toad," which pleased her vastly, as she had reason to consider it an excellent sign for his temper. But after all, when she was breathing freely, and thinking of topics to talk about, he jumped up as if something had stabbed him, and went plunging through the door, before she had time to put in another word of protest.

His mother sat looking miserable for a short

time, and then went out also, and a little way up the road to where a knot of neighbours were gathered, some seated in the dwindling shadow of the Sheridans' walls, and some in the broad sunshine on the top of the dyke. The sky was still clear and deeply ultramarine, but had lost its earlier glistening, as of suspended dews, and looked sultry. Low down on its southern rim the jagged edge of a dense black cloud would just show itself here and there for a moment, and shrink back out of ken. You might have fancied some huge dark-hided shape lurking there in ambush, and as it prowled to and fro, ever and anon inadvertently discovering a pricked-up ear or ridge of spine. About the Sheridans' door people were carrying on a conversation leisurely and intermittently; perhaps one should say a series of conversations, so long were the frequent pauses. The flow of their discourse quickened into animation and continuity only in some eddy of anecdote; as, for example, when Ody Rafferty was recounting a fracas which had taken place lately somewhere between down below and down beyant.

"Pat Martin was tellin' me," he said, "young Willy Molloy and another young fellow from Drumesk, be the name of Joyce, were after havin' the greatest set-to at all on Tuesday night where they were workin' for Sullivan. Ploughin' for turnips young Molloy was, and dhruv over as tone in the furrow, and smashed a back-band all to flitterjigs; whereby Sullivan came along and gave him dog's abuse. So Molloy ups and sez Joyce had a right to ha' seen the plough-harness was sound afore they went out; and Joyce he ups and sez the harness was right enough, and the other had no call to be forcin' his plough over such a sizeable lump of a stone. So from that they got to bullyraggin' and bargin' one another outrageous, till the end of it was they fell to boxin' on the road goin' home most terrific. And young Molloy got the other chap down, and Pat sez he'd have had him choked as sure as there was breath' in his body, on'y ould Molly Finny caught him be the hind leg, till some of the rest of them pulled him off. Och, he said it was a great fight entirely."

"The on'y wonder is," said Mrs. Sheridan, "that them young chaps don't do slaughter on aich other oftener than happens."

"That puts me in mind of one of the further-backest things I remimber," said Joe Ryan, old Mick's youngest brother. "'Twas as long ago as when I wasn't the size of them spalpeens over there —Look at them now; sure the divil's busy wid them; they're draggin' a couple of chuckens up and down the street in their mother's saucepan; just let her git home to them. Sure I dunno what ould ages ago it mayn't be, for it's generations since the Macrans quit out of this, and it was the time they had the Quigleys' house. But I mind the son Luke one Sunday mornin' comin' up here from where iver he'd been; powerful hot weather it was, and much about this saison of the year. And when he come, his ould father and sisters and some more of us were just streelin' about the place permiscuous, so he streeled along too, and nobody noticed anythin' oncommon. Well, we were passin' be the dyke there at the bottom of Mrs. M'Gurk's field of pitaties, and in one corner of it there was a great blaze like of red poppies, as there may be this present instiant for that matter. But when Luke Macran set eyes on them, he let the most surprisin' yell you iver witnessed, and grabbed hould of his father, as he might ha' done and he scared at anythin' afore he was grown 'Lord in heaven,' sez he, pointin' afore him, 'what's that there?' 'Sure what else 'ud it be, you gomeral,' sez one of the girls, 'excipt a clump of poppies?' 'Troth,' sez he, 'I dunno what I thought it was at all,' and began laughin' a great horse-laugh, as if he was thryin' to pass it off. So we walked on a few perches till we come where there was a line of poppies agin, growin' in the long grass under the dyke: and if we did, Luke Macran let another yell out of him you might have heard in Cork, and stood starin' wild. Sez he: 'The divil's done that on me; the divil's done that on me. It's on this road, and it's all along the other road—and where am I to git to out of it? Where am I to git to at all, I say?' sez he, seemin' to go altogether beyond himself; and wid that he lep' the dyke—'twas just there at the road-corner —and away wid him out over the bog as if Hell was let loose behind him. Faith, he whirrelled through wet and dry like an ould rag caught in a strong wind. Folk thought he had drink taken. But maybe somethin' better than half an hour after he'd gone, the pólis came up wid word there was a man lyin' under a bank in a bit o' bog Sallinbeg ways—on Hilfirthy's land it was—and his head all battered to smithereens wid the handle of an ould graip; and he seen alive last in company wid Luke Macran—drinkin' together they were the night before. Och, that was an ugly business; nothin' 'ud suit me but to skyte off down there to see what I could. Howanc'er, the misfortnit bein' niver was took. I dunno what became of him at all, and his family. Quite dacint poor people they were, on'y Luke did always be fiery-hot in his temper. Sure, I daresay you might remimber it, Judy; we're much the one age."

"Bedad do I," said Judy; "it had slipped hould of me recollections, but now you mintion it I remimber it right well. But it's a misapperhension to say nobody noticed aught amiss wid him, for the first instiant he came you might aisy see he was thrimblin' head and fut like a horse that's after takin' a fright, and his eyes were that wild—the look of him's as clare before me yit as if he was standin' as close to me as Mrs. Doyne is now. Isn't there e'er a seat in it for you, ma'am? You don't look anyways fit to be standin' about; 'deed it's mighty indifferint you're lookin' whativer. Pat, set the ould creepy stool for Mrs. Doyne."

"No, thank you, ma'am," said Mrs. Doyne, "I'm just steppin' in to spake to Mrs. Kilfoyle. 'Tis the hate of the sun discommodes me; it's blazin' hot this day."

"'Twon't trouble her much longer then, if that's what ails her," said Peter Sheridan, as she turned away; "'twill be black out on us afore we're five minyits oulder. There'll be little enough hate left in it onst it gits behind that."

. "That" was an enormous blue-black cloud-rampart with crenellated summit and buttressed base, which had reared itself almost to the zenith in the north, and still rose steadily. Livid white cloudlets scudded across its dark face, and here and there a rift let in a background of coppery glare. "Thunder," everybody said or thought; and straightway anxious forebodings about potatoes and clutches of eggs mixed in many minds with a vaguer disquietude. Lisconnel is seriously alarmed at thunderstorms. "It might pass off yit," Judy Ryan said hopefully. "That's not the way of the win'. What trifle there is does be southerly."

"As if," Peter Sheridan rejoined ominously, "everybody didn't know that thunder comes up agin the win', which is of a piece wid the rest of its contrariness—and bad cess to the same."

Still, the sun held Mrs. Doyne in a scorching dazzle all the way to the Kilfoyles' door, so that she had finished thanking Mrs. Kilfoyle kindly for the griddle-bread, before her blinking eyes had caught sight of the little old woman in her obscure corner. Mrs. Doyne, a down-hearted person, whose experience of life had not been calculated to encourage her, was always very capable of fears, which she sometimes kept to herself for private brooding over, but generally sooner or later communicated to a sympathising neighbour. Therefore Mrs. Kilfoyle was not at all surprised when her visitor now sat down and said lamentably: "Me heart's broke." This is our customary formula for announcing that we are in any sort of tribulation, and may mean nothing serious.

"Are you findin' yourself took worse agin, me dear?" said Mrs. Kilfoyle, commiseratingly.

"Ah no," said Mrs. Doyne, "it's the lads, Terence

and Matt; they have me distracted. I dunno what's come over them this while back, for they always lived togither as frindly as a pair of ould brogues, but now there's somethin' gone agin them. They're that cross wid one another 'twould dishearten you to see. Niver a thing Matt can do but Terence 'll find fau't wid it, and they'll bicker and allegate about every hand's turn; I believe they'd raise an argufyment about the stars in the sky, if they could find nothin' else handier; and I dunno where it'll ind."

"Sure most people do be contráry that way now and agin," said Mrs. Kilfoyle consolingly, "and nobody can expect young lads like them to have a scrumption of sinse."

"That's where it is; for how can you tell what deminted thing they'll be apt to go do? Why sure, if one of them lost control of himself for an instiant of time, he might be hittin' the other a crack he'd niver git the better of, before he knew what he was at. Och, the dread of that's niver out of me mind, when they're away togither. I do be hearin' somebody comin' down the road wid the news every fut that stirs. And I can't sleep at night for thinkin' of it. Often I'm wishin' the day 'ud niver come round agin to be givin' thim a chanst of desthroyin' one another. 'Let it keep dark,' sez I, 'for there's little to see be daylight but what one's afeard to look at.'"

"Now that's the talk of a fool," said Mrs. Kilfoyle with candour, "but my opinion is, nobody's rightly sinsible in the nights. The notions they'll take in their heads when they're lyin' awake are mostly as onraisonable as when they're dramin' outright. If I were you, Mrs. Doyne, ma'am, I'd not mind a thraneen what I thought in the nights, onless it was as a pattron for thinkin' somethin' diffrint by otherwhiles. Faix, if some one was kilt every time a couple of people were onplisant in their tempers, how many of us 'ud be left alive?"

"It's not *every* time, it's just the one time I go in dread of," said Mrs. Doyne, "and I know Matt's out on the bog cuttin' turf this mornin', and before I came in to you Terence went off there wid himself too. As like as not they'll git disputin' about somethin', and the wild bog's a terrible dangerous place for any persons to be quarrellin' in, among all them higeous deep bottomless houles. Sure a slip or a shove might sind one of them over the edge, and they tussellin' about convanient. And then there do be the loys and graips lyin' around—supposin' either of them caught up such a thing into his hand in a rage—och, the saints shield them! And it's as black and as bitter as sut Terence, poor crathur was lookin' when I last set eyes on him."

"Talkin' of black," said Mrs. Kilfoyle, with intentional inconsequence, "it seems to me growin' onnatural dark."

The thickest shadows, indeed, had stolen forth from all the room-corners, emboldened by the abrupt withdrawal of the long rays, which had thrust a wedge of glowing gold in at the open door, and turned Mrs. Kilfoyle's favourite metallic burnished jug into a refulgent star where it hung in its remote recess. The two women rose, and stood looking out on a great gloom.

People who have never seen a wide sweep of bogland beneath the scowl of a thunder-cloud, hardly know what blackness the face of the earth can gather at noontide. Nowhere else, one imagines, does mirk swooping from overhead so mingle with mirk striking up from underfoot, for the ground seems not merely to passively accept the shadows flung down upon it, but to reflect them back, as water reflects sunshine. The grim bog broadens and flattens itself under the louring cloud-masses, as if some monstrous weight were actually drawn across it, and their blackness is thrown into relief by lurid gleams of smoky yellow. To-day the sullen lustreless glare, as from the lowe of some far-distant furnace, seemed to beat against the dense vapour-screen and struggle through its interstices with an evil-looking glimmer.

"Wirra," said Mrs. Kilfoyle, "woman alive, did

you iver behould the like of such a sky as that? It might be a loughful of coal-tar boilin' up over an ould brass pan. The Lord be good to us this day, but there's goin' to be somethin' beyant the beyants entirely. If it was the end of all the ages, it couldn't look more onnatural."

Mrs. Doyne was ordinarily much more afraid of thunder-storms than Mrs. Kilfoyle, who had a reassuring theory that if you just stayed *quite* in whatever place you happened to be, the lightning would know where you were, and be apt to keep out of your way. "Liker," Ody Rafferty objected, "a mad dog that won't turn out of the road he's started runnin' in to bite you." But Mrs. Kilfoyle said it was all one. Lisconnel is decidedly eclectic in its philosophical explanations of natural phenomena. On this occasion, however, Mrs. Doyne's mind had been preoccupied by an anxiety that crowded out her usual panic, and when she strained her gaze over the expanse of gloom before her, it was not to note the march of the menaced storm. " Katty," she said to a little Kilfoyle who stood near, "you that have the good sight, look and tell me can you see aught movin' yonder on the bog." Katty's grey eyes were as keen as any young hawk's, and she at once replied: " Matt Doyne's cuttin' turf away down there, and his brother's crossin' over to where he is; he's just after leppin' a bit of a pool." As she spoke, a faint waft of wind came panting towards them out of the breathless hush, and made all the taller grass-tufts tremble. "Here it is," said Mrs. Kilfoyle solemnly; but nothing followed except a slight puff of dust. Mrs. Doyne said with a groan, "Och, them two lads!"

"Sure they'll run home in next to no time; nary a harm they'll git. Why, gossoons like them just put down their heads and off wid them skytin' across all before them. Eh, but it doesn't seem so long," said the little old woman, ' since I'd be doin' the same meself. They're not like you and me, that must be liftin' our feet over aich separate stick or stone in our road same as a couple of ould hins. Mercy be among us, woman dear, you're niver goin' after them in the face of that?"—for Mrs. Doyne was gathering the folds of her ragged shawl under her chin with her left hand, which, if you wear a shawl habitually, means that you are setting out somewhere. "It's not a right thing for you to be doin' at all, gittin' yourself drownded dead for nothin' in the polthers of rain we're safe to have presintly, if there's nought worse than polthers comin'."

"Terence was mad, I know, about Matt cuttin at that turf-bank," murmured Mrs. Doyne, glancing nervously at the darkest cloud.

"Git out," said Mrs. Kilfoyle, "is it ravin' frantic you suppose them to be, that they'd stop there risin' rows about turf-cuttin', wid the noon-day turned as black as the inside of an ould sut-bag before their eyes? They'd have more—Whooo— goodness save and deliver us all!"

A vibrant steely glare sawed the gloom before their faces for a terrible moment, and the thunder-peal, almost overtaking it, prolonged their affright through a sharp rattle and bellowing boom, dying away in lumbering rumbles and thuds. "Run in, Katty, run in, both of yous!" cried Mrs. Kilfoyle, vanishing into her doorway. But Mrs. Doyne darted straight across the road, and out upon the scowling bog.

She went in mortal fear. Weak as she was, the mere solitary traversing of so much rough unsheltered ground would have seemed formidable to her; but now if the swaying cloud-bastions had been a fort sweeping her path with shot and shell until the torn air round her shrieked death, she could not have found it harder to face. Every foot she set before the other had in a mental debate been turned to flee ere the step was taken forwards. As she walked over the yielding ling-stalks and slippery short grass, she dared not lift her eyes from the ground lest they should meet that fearsome flickering blaze. It came again and again, making her heart stand still with terror, but a dread within dread still drove her on, muttering broken appeals to all the powers of heaven. Then the air hissed, and she felt hailstones pelting on her forehead and hands, and presently saw them gathering in white drifts under black roots and banks, and sprinkling dark spaces of bare turf. Cold blasts came with the hail, flapping her shawl into her eyes; they seemed to be suffocating her, yet when they had blustered by, she felt as if they had taken her breath with them. She could hardly tell the real thunder-claps from the sounds that surged and hummed in her ears, and her knees began to give at each heavily stumbling step, like a stalk of meadow-grass when its joint-knot is snapped. Worse still, a sense grew upon her that all these things had happened to her before, an uncanny feeling, which brings desperation with it. This sense strengthened suddenly when at last, coming, as she thought, near the place where her boys had been seen, she forced herself to look up, and at once descried them through the hurtle of the pelting shower, only a few yards distant—and fighting. Terence was trying to wrest a spade out of Matt's hand. For one nightmare moment she stood spell-stopped; the next, she was endeavouring wildly to call to them, but she believed that no sound passed her lips. Only from somewhere far off in the dimness a strange hoarse voice seemed to shriek meaninglessly. And before she could struggle on again, floods of seething darkness rushed in upon her from all sides, and swept her out of consciousness.

Mrs. Doyne was mistaken. Her cry came distinctly to her sons, and stopped their scuffle as effectually as if they had been separated by an explosion. "Was that mother callin'?" they said simultaneously, standing with dropped arms; and in the same instant they saw her fall. "Oh, my God! oh, my God! she's struck," Matt shouted. Terence was speechless, and put all his energies into a great spring, foiled by a twisted heather-root, which tripped him up, so that he had to crawl dragging a useless foot after him to the place where his brother had forestalled him in white-lipped distraction. Neither of them could doubt that she was dead, but Terence yelled to Matt to run home for his life and get help; and Matt fled away through a blinding blue glare, with the thunder-roll trampling after him overhead.

Then Terence sat down on a low grassy ledge, and said to his mother: "Och, you bad ould one, what made you go for to be stravadin' about the bog this sort of weather? Sure 'twas no thing to go do. But I daresay you're better now to be lyin' as quite as you can, till some of them comes to lend you a hand home; for you see I'm after wrenchin' me fool of a fut.—Did you say anythin', mother? What was you sayin'? Musha now, but you're the great ould villin to be lettin' on there, thinkin' to tirrify me. Sure I'm always tellin' you you're no better than a rael downright rogue, wid the invintions of you. Howsome'er, maybe all the same I won't let the hailstones be hoppin' in your face.— The divil tear me that I wouldn't stop in the house wid her this mornin'. What's gone at all wid Matt and the lads, that there's ne'er a sign of them comin' along?—Did you hear that clap, mother? Didn't you then? It was a fine one intirely, if you'd been listenin'. But you needn't be mindin', for we'll just help you home out of it in next to no time, y'ould villin.—If the lads iver come."

They did come as fast as they could, and carried her home through the storm to her black little doorway, which seemed as much to her present purpose as a palace of marble and ivory. Several people set out in quest of the priest and the doctor, and Dan O'Beirne, whom it was feared they would not find, he being supposed absent from home, and the others devoted themselves to the discussion of the case in all its bearings. Little else remained for them to do. But they decided that Mrs. Doyne, whatever might ha' took her, had not been struck by lightning. For Ody Rafferty had been told by a farmer, who had had a heifer destroyed in that way, that the crathur was all blackened on one side like the stem of a burnt furze-bush, and there were no signs of any such thing on Mrs. Doyne. It was liker parlissis. Everybody speculated, too, about " what she could ha' been doin' out there on the bog, and she scarce fit to go the lenth of her own shadow "—everybody except Mrs. Kilfoyle, who was merciful, and said sure maybe the crathur, Heaven help her, had been lookin' for one of the lads to run on an errand for her.

Terence, unhappily for himself, could run on no errand ; and he had sat for a very long time on the dyke near his door, perforce overhearing the neighbours determine what his mother had died of, when Peg Sheridan limped up to him with a poor scrap of comfort. Peg has, as it may be remembered, a serious trouble of her own, which makes her neighbours' affairs rather insipid to her under ordinary circumstances, so that she is not generally popular, since sensitive people will condone many deliberate sins more easily than the unintentional affront of a simple friendly indifference. But they allow that if anything off the common ails them, there is no one readier than Peg to do them any good turn she can ; the presence of a great grief, in fact, filling her with sympathy, as a forgotten rock-pool is filled when a wave from the wide sea flaps over its brim. She came towards Terence more jerkily than usual, for the frequent flashes scared her as much as anybody, and complicated her chronic hobble with queer swerves and startings aside; and she said: "Terence, I don't believe she's *that* bad. I saw her somethin' the same way one day last harvest, when she had Stacey like one deminted, but niver a die on her that time, or maybe this aither, if we could git Dan O'Beirne to her soon enough."

"Peg," said Terence, looking up into her face, where freckles and sunburn had not found much beauty to spoil, "you're the jewel of the world, so you are, to be sayin' it. But she's gone—and she was axin' me to stay wid her."

That day's storm raged long and ranged widely. It met a detachment of the Lisconnel congregation on their way back from Mass, and so daunted them that they took shelter under the wall of Dan O'Beirne's forge; they could not get inside, because the place was all shut up, and he had gone somewhere, probably on shebeening business. Stacey Doyne was among them, somewhat out of spirits. Her expedition had been, on the whole, a disappointment. It is true that she had attended Mass, which was what she thought had been her object, and yet—However, it certainly was no affair of hers, nor did she care a thraneen, who spoke to the Farrelly girls as they went into the porch, or who was not there to give her "good morning" when she came out. She daresaid, besides, that she looked a quare ugly ould show in her patched petticoat and torn shawl, and considered that she would probably stay at home next Sunday.

As the rain long continued to come down in gleaming sheets, which the other women would call the clearing shower and just wait a bit to see the end of, she grew uneasy about her mother, who she knew would be fretting herself into fiddle-strings, and perhaps would run out in the wet to fill the pot, and get her death of cold on them, unless she was too badly frighted of the thunder. But they were starting at last, when a Duffclane lad ran against them as they came round the angle of the forge wall. " Is Himself in it?" he shouted. "Och no, I was sartin-sure he wasn't. He's wanted up above. I met young Mick Ryan leggin' it over the bog about Shanasheen to look for him. And Stacey Doyne's wid you—Och Stacey, it's bad news I'm bringin' you—och your poor mother's distroyed, girl alive—burnt black. In the fire? Not at all—wid the awful lightnin'—shtruck down at her door, and burnt to a cinder in an instiant. One of the young chaps was shtruck too—blinded —but there's life in him yit, and I'm goin' to thry can I git Father Rooney to him—I must be steppin'."

Stacey thought at first that when she had run

all those miles home without stopping, and had found her mother sitting in the corner by the hearth saying, "Child of grace, what's kep' you till this time?" she would stay there content all the rest of her life, and never again put herself in the way of hearing people bawl such things at her. But by the time she had run herself out of breath, she had run into the heart of a blank despair. She walked slower then and slower amid the unmeaning murmur of eager voices, and splashing rain and distant thunder, and towards the end of their journey she lagged so that the other girls pulled her along between them. When they were coming in sight of their knockawn, somebody exclaimed, "Why look you, isn't that Dan O'Beirne himself and young Dan on the top of the hill?" and with that they all made a rush for the latest news. Stacey slipped behind, and sat down under a trickling, lichened boulder, with her hands over eyes and ears to crush out sights and sounds.

She sat down in a condemned cell of misery, and she rose to her feet, if one must not say in the courts of Paradise, at any rate somewhere in its purlieus. Because young Dan, who had pulled away her hands from her face, was still holding her wrist and cheerfully saying: "Sure she's doin' finely now, Stacey dear; you've no need to be disthressin' yourself about her. She wasn't too bad at all. 'Twas just a wakeness she took, and me father gave her some oi his stuff done her a power o' good, Stacey jewel."

The very skies had cleared swiftly, and sent a sheaf of long westering rays to kindle the rainbow fire in a myriad shimmering drops.

"Ay," corroborated the elder Dan, "she'll be as lively as a grig to-morrow, plase God. Terence 'll be longer laid up wid the bit of a wranch he's after givin' his ankle."

"Thank you kindly, Dan; sure they had me annoyed," was all Stacey said.

"Where'd the whoule of us be on'y for Dan?" said the widow M'Gurk.

Dan O'Beirne, the blacksmith and shebeener, is so well liked by his neighbours, that they all are perfectly certain his grandfather, also a blacksmith, used to forge pikeheads in the troubles of '98. His own peculiar source of pride is that his family belongs to the O'Beirnes of Wicklow, who, as everybody knows, have been notorious rebels time out of mind. But that his popularity does not rest upon these historical bases will be clear to any of us who are aware how many miles he will tramp unfee'd to visit some one "took sick," with whom, if bad enough, he thinks it a small matter to sit up all night. His broad benevolent forehead has glimmered like a lamp of hope between mud floor and thatch roof through many a dark hour; and if, as not seldom happens, all the light flickers out when the day is dawning, everybody knows that Dan left nothing undone that lay within the compass of his kindliness and skill.

"Bedad, if Dan O'Beirne couldn't keep the breath in her body, the Divil himself couldn't, not if the one was her sowl, and the other was purgatory," Pat Ryan said on an occasion of this sort, using a figure of speech which perhaps had more appositeness than he suspected.

Dan's merits, scientific and moral, are indeed highly rated, not only absolutely but relatively, as contrasted with those of Dr. Ward at the dispensary down beyant, whose services Lisconnel seeks rarely, and generally in vain, his district being a world too wide for any licensed practitioner to administer single-handed, however swift his rattle-trap car, and however brief his visits. When he proves thus unattainable, people remark: "Ah well, I question could he ha' done a hap'orth of good." He is a well-manin' poor man, they say, and mightn't make such a bad offer at it, if he wasn't always in a hurry, and would take time to what he was about. But it stands to reason that he can't know rightly what he's doing, when he won't so much as be at the trouble of attending to half the particulars his patients give him about their symptoms, and interrupts them in the middle, as if he could possibly find out how they were feeling without being told. As for his medicines, they have no strength in them at all—Lisconn utterly despises any physic that is in the least endurable either in taste or odour—or if he does send an odd bottle that smells as if it might have some good in it, he calls it a *Linyeemeni*, and is careful to stick on a yellow poison label, for fear you should try a drop. On the other hand, there is plenty of strength in his language, if by chance he attends a summons, and finds the invalid in a normal state of health. His frame of mind when such a *contretemps* takes place is afterwards variously described as " ragin' mad "—" as cross as the dogs "—" fit to be tied "—" on his hind legs begob "—and so forth. " As if," Brian Kilfoyle remarked, " he'd liefer ha' found the unlucky bosthoon lyin' on the broad of his back waitin' death ; or as if it worn't as simple and aisy as anythin' else to say ' The divil take yous,' and rowl off home agin, wid no trouble perscribin' or aught." ' And be ped for it too, mind you, handsome," appended a neighbour.

This is in striking contrast to Dan O'Beirne, who, when called in by mistake, will say quite plisant. " Sure I'd niver be wishful to see you worser anyways," or declare it would take an

M.D. with more letters than he had to his name to perceive much amiss, which gives an agreeably humorous complexion to affairs. And Dan's medicines are undeniably strong. A certain "corjil" of his own compounding enjoys a very wide local reputation, and has "brought round" dozens and scores of people. If questioned about its ingredients, he will but grin blandly, and say something of the nature of, "Och now, that 'ud be tellin'"; however, anybody can tell that it smells aromatically of herbs. My own opinion is that the rest of it consists mainly of faith and potheen, though in what proportions they are combined, I am not chemist enough to discover.

At all events there can be no doubt that on this thundery Sunday afternoon a sup of it out of her thick pink-and-white delft cup, with embossed coral-sprays on the sides, materially helped to restore poor Mrs. Doyne, who began to feebly struggle back from her long swoon or trance, just as Dan and his son, by some neatly-joined pieces of good luck, arrived at her door. So rapidly did she revive, that he was soon able to pronounce her iligant and grand, and to diagnose her case as "just some quare turn the ugly weather'd been after givin' her. But, glory be to goodness, she'd find herself complately the better of it by to-morra or next day." Outside her door, however, he said with emphasis: "Ay, she'll do rightly. But she's wake these times, the poor woman, faible, I might say; and if she's torminted wid anythin', or gave frights to, or botherationed wid folks risin' argyfyments about blathers and nonsinse, there's no sayin' but she might be slippin' away wid herself suddint on yous, one of these fine days. She just might, and so I tell you plainly;" which makes me think that Mrs. Kilfoyle may have dropped him a hint. Then, when Dan had prescribed a stupe of marshmallows for Terence's sprain, his professional duties were discharged, and he was at liberty to indulge himself and his neighbours with more lively conversation.

It really seemed as if the electrical condition of the atmosphere must have given a fillip to the march of events in and around Lisconnel, so much more than usual happened thereabouts on that day. "Who do you think are after makin' a match of it?" Dan said towards the end of his budget of news; "it was only settled this mornin', the young chap was tellin' me, and we comin' along. Why, Maggie Farrelly, no less, and a farmer's son from off one of the Inishes, a young man of the name of M'Grenaghan, and a dacint lad I'm tould. If they're the people I'm supposin', they own cows. Maybe he's got no great prize wid her, not but what she's well-lookin' enough. I'd not go for to say anythin' too bad agin the girl, but in my opinion she's a bit of a rogue. Over fond of keepin' the lads fandanglin' after her, to be makin' fools of them, accordin' as she may fancy. Och, very belike she might settle down now that she's sorted out one for herself, on'y I'd as lief as not she'd no dalins wid any belongins of mine. D'you know, a while ago I had a notion she was thinkin' —where's Dan got to? Sure is that him above there lookin' out over the road?—I'd a notion she was thinkin' of gittin' round him, for I noticed him goin' about wid her followin' a couple of times or so. But he swears be this and be that there was ne'er a talk of any such a thing on his part. 'Twas a frind of his was about coortin' her, and axed him to keep around and be slippin' in a word now and agin might give her mind a sort of slant to begin wid. That was foolish enough too, in all conscience, to be for slinkin' in on another's lad's tongue, instead of spakin' up and biddin' the girl to take him or lave him on his own recommindations. Any way, the end of the matter is that she's sacked her ould sweethearts, ivery man jack of them, and took up wid this one, she hadn't set eyes on, they say, a couple of weeks since."

"Musha then, ould Horny himself might take Mag Farrelly and welcome, for me," said Terence Doyne, who was so exhilarated by the reaction of his escape from despair to security, that it was all his lamed foot could do to keep him from dancing.

"Or for me," said his brother Matt, who also felt at peace with all the world, "and the whoule lot of them into the bargain. They're mostly more bother than they're worth—a dale. I'll go and be gittin' some of the mallow for his fut, and Stacey can give it a boil when she comes home. She'll be here directly."

"Whethen Maggie Farrelly, indeed!" said Judy Ryan, who had as she said herself, "no opinion," by which she meant a bad one, of the bride-elect. "Cock her up wid a fine young man like your son Dan! He's got more wit than to look the side of road she is, I'll go bail. There's not one of those Farrellys I'd give you the black of me eye for; a slutherin', deceptionable set."

Soon after this, the elder Dan joined his son upon the hill, and they fared homewards, presently falling in, as we have seen, with a party of friends. It would, indeed, have been rather inhuman to keep Stacey Doyne so long upon the road as I have done, were it not that she was all the while in Paradise, where people overlook such trivialities as being wet through and tired out with a many miles' tramp, and having had nothing to eat for nearly a round of the clock.

"And how at all did you hear tell of it, Dan,"

inquired Mrs. M'Gurk, "when nobody had an idea where to be lookin' for you, and one's liker to lose one's self than to find any one else around on the bog, if one goes chancin' it?"

"'Twas the young chap," said Dan, pointing to his son; "he met wid a couple of spalpeens inquirin' for me not far from our place, and he happint to know I was gone Loughgaula ways to spake to a man, so he legged it after me there, but I'd quit out of that afore he came, and then he follied me on to Brosnakill, where he got me. So he's had great runnin' over the counthry this day, the young rapscallion."

"Troth," said young Dan, "I'd run twyst that far for Stacey Doyne any day of the year, or for any one belongin' to her. And she knows it."

No declaration could, according to Lisconnel canons, have been more explicitly worded. It startled them all severely, young Dan himself not excepted. If Stacey had shown herself by any means equal to the occasion, she would at least have responded: "Know it, sez he! Bedad and indeed it's himself has the wonerful notions about what I may happin to know. Sure he's just talkin' foolish." But she was taken somewhat at a disadvantage, and in fact said nothing at all.

"Tare-an-ages!" said Dan's father, "and is that the way of the win' with you? Well tubbe sure, but ther's no bein' up to the likes of you. Begorrah, I might ha' known he'd somethin' in his head when he was runnin' me off of me misfortnit ould legs all the way over from yonder to here this mornin'. I'd as lief ha' been in leadin' strings to an unruly bullock. Not that I'm denyin' he might aisy ha' took up wid some one worser. There's no dacinter people on this counthry side than the Doynes, and little Stacey — How-an-e'er Mrs. M'Gurk, we that have the wit are to be pitied now, aren't we? wid them young gomerals—the crathurs."

Old Dan's chagrin was about half earnest, his inordinate pride in his handsome son compelling him to think but poorly of anybody considered as a possible daughter-in-law, while his general philanthropy disposed him to make the best of everybody that came in his way, none the less when appearing in the shape of a pretty, pleasant-spoken slip of a colleen, with whom he had been acquainted ever since she was big enough to crawl out of her door at him as he passed. The result of these conflicting tendencies here was a vacillation between censoriousness and indulgence, which made it difficult for him to preserve a consistent demeanour. "I'll tell you one thing, and that's not two," he said, with a sudden access of resolution caused by a glance around him, " we'd better all of us be steppin' home, if we've had enough of dhrownding to satisfy us for this day. The sky's cloudin' over agin, like as if the storm might be plannin' to give us another bout. Begob now, Dan, there's no call for you to be seein' Stacey over the hill. The child's in a hurry to run home to her mother, and you'd just delay her. Forby, don't I know as well as if I was inside you, that you'll be takin' off wid yourself over here the first thing to-morra ; so where's the sinse of bidin' for a wettin' to-night ? There's a sun-dog over yonder agin that black cloud, and look at them crathurs crawlin', you may say, on their wings ; there's nary a surer sign of rain."

The swallows, " preying towards storms," were indeed flying very low, sweeping in such immense circles that their return seemed as problematical as the re-appearance of a periodic comet. Darkly piled up cloud-masses still hovered and drifted, spreading deep purple shadows over the bog, gloom folded on gloom, ready to league with the gathering twilight. But just as Stacey turned to run home, the sun, now dropped very far down in the west, found a little round hole in a grim black wall, and through it flashed up obliquely a jet of golden-amber fire, broadening fanwise sheer across the sky. It set all the raindrops twinkling, where every leaf and blade had its drop ; and it glistened and shimmered in many a brimming pool. Speeding down the hill, Stacey felt as if she were flying into an enchanted, dazzling sort of world on new and wonderful wings. A neighbour of hers, however, who was sedately going the same way, observed : " It looks bad for the weather when the sun makes a chimney like yon ; we'll be apt to have a wet night." And another replied : " I doubt we're not done wid the thunder yit."

CHAPTER VIII.

BETWEEN TWO LADY DAYS.

THE Lady Day in harvest, which fell six weeks or so after that electrical July Sunday, was splendidly fine in Lisconnel, steeped through and through with ripe August sunshine, and unruffled by any restless breeze. Its serene beauty jarred upon Stacey Doyne's mood, and, though she did not guess, helped to make the lag-foot hours halt by more slowly and heavily. But she was keenlier alive to a sense of aggravating circumstances when, at an early period of the morning, it became evident that Mad Bell, seized by one of her irresistible lyrical frenzies, had been driven to establish herself on a sun-smitten bank near her door, whence her shrill singing resounded far and wide. What she sang loudest and longest was a favourite ditty beginning:

> "Before I was married, I used to dhrink tay,
> But since I am married, 'tis buttermilk-whey;
> Before I was married, I sat in the parlour,
> But since I am married, 'tis in the ash-corner."

A wish to escape beyond the range of that oft-repeated air led Stacey to ramble away further than she otherwise would have done over the heathery crests of the knockawn, where the sombre ruddy bloom against the black peat-mould suggested the smouldering and charring of half-extinguished embers, until at last she sat down on a boulder between two sheltering clumps of broom and furze, which made her a low-roofed bower. Here Mad Bell was too far off for the tune or words; only a faint skirl came fitfully, borne upon a flagging breeze, scarcely "a trace," as chemists say, upon the surrounding atmosphere of stillness. Nothing else broke it either with motion or sound, except when, ever and anon, a flight of little wild birds got up suddenly in the distance, like a handful of dust tossed into the air, and when a curlew cried plaintively across the bog, a cunning tone-poet, who can set a whole landscape to melancholy in one quick chromatic phrase.

Stacey wanted, indeed, no external incitements to sadness, having at present ample grounds for it in her own situation and reflections. This radiant summer morning, with its arch of moteless sapphire and high-tides of unstinted shining, should have ushered in her wedding-day. It had all been arranged weeks ago—ages ago it seemed to her now—for the elder Dan's dissatisfaction with his son's choice had melted away rapidly and completely. In point of fact, on that very eventful Sunday evening, when the matter first came to light, the two O'Beirnes had on their homeward way met the Cross Priest posting up to Lisconnel in obedience to a tragical summons, and in the course of the explanations which ensued, the good-natured blacksmith betrayed himself into tacitly withdrawing any meditated opposition to the match.

"So, your Riverence, there's little signs of a buryin' over this business at all, at all," said he, "but I wouldn't say as much consarnin' a weddin'. Troth no I'd not. For to tell your Riverence the truth, it's my belief that young gomeral there has a notion—himself and little Stacey Doyne—to be troublin' you, or Father Rooney—long life to him —one of these days. Och begorrah, that's the worth of the likes of them "—Dan privately thought that the three kingdoms would have been "put to it" to produce the likes of his son—" what better need you expec'?"

Father Carroll was humane enough to hear with relief that, after all, none of his parishioners had been burnt alive or blinded, and he naturally rejoiced at the abridgment of his long late ride. So he received the news more genially than usual, and as he turned his horse's willing head, he shook his whip-handle jocularly at young Dan, saying

"Indeed now, O'Beirne, I wouldn't put it past them, the pair of them. But if you're for setting up a wife, Dan, you'll have to be steady, and stick to your work, and mind what you're about. Clap on your blinkers, me lad, and keep the road straight before you, or you'll land more than yourself in the ditch."

Dan, who looked very unwontedly sheepish, kicked a lump of turf in front of him further than his own shadow, which stretched a long way distortedly through the beams of the rising moon, as he answered: "Och, sure me father wouldn't git his health if he didn't be talkin', so he wouldn't. Be the hoky, it's a won'erful man he is for romancin' intirely."

After this, the current of the young couple's affairs, so far as they stood upon the choice of friends, was practically unimpeded; and their wooing undoubtedly deserved the benison pronounced on those which are conducted with despatch. But the edict of destiny fulfils itself in many ways. At the time when young Dan entered into his engagement with Stacey Doyne, he had a prior one on hand, which his new tie did not dispose, or rather forbade, him to break. This was a journey all the way up to the county Antrim, where a friend of his held out prospects of a four weeks' job at a compressed peat manufactory, the manager of which found labour scarce in those harvesting days. Now young Dan O'Beirne being not only strong and stalwart, but endowed with an intuitive gift for understanding the "quareness" of all sorts of machinery, Thomas M'Crum, the northerner, who had himself got the promise of work up there, made no manner of doubt that so desirable a hand would find at all events temporary employment, and a scale of remuneration which sounded prodigious in the ears of Lisconnel. Dan's contemplated marriage rendered the acquisition of a little ready-money in a high degree expedient, if not absolutely necessary; for his father's philanthropy was of an humble personal kind, never known to enrich or in any way aggrandise the family in which it runs, and the O'Beirnes, despite forge and shebeen, were hardly better off than their struggling neighbours. Given a pound or two in hand for the purchase of "a few odd sticks of things," and the rent of a cabin down below, Dan and Stacey could start housekeeping with light hearts; failing that, the match would be held imprudent even by people who entertained the most moderate views about marriage settlements. So Dan went off one morning, confident of returning with at least that sum a clear fortnight before Lady Day, which had been fixed for the wedding.

Stacey had plenty to distract her mind during

his absence. There was the trousseau, for one thing. Her mother sold their pig prematurely, at somewhat of a sacrifice, that she might be able to buy a sufficiency of hideous strong brown wincey for a body and a skirt. These two articles of clothing are seldom simultaneously acquired in Lisconnel. And when, in the course of the negotiations at his shop in the Town, Mr. Corr learned the purpose for which the stuff was required, he added gratis some yards of the stoutest grey holland in his stock to make Stacey a couple of large aprons—*praskeens* she called them. Whereupon Lisconnel opined that Mr. Corr always was a kind-hearted poor man. Then the wedding itself furnished a theme for endless planning and discussion, especially when Farmer Hilfirthy, down below, actually promised the loan of his jaunting-car to meet the bridal party at Classon's Boreen, half-way to the chapel. Stacey had never in her life been on a car or any other vehicle, and the prospect of the drive evidently heightened more than one would have imagined, her sense of the solemnity and importance of the whole ceremony.

Thus the days bustled on blithely enough, burnished up for her by the gleams of a happy hour which she knew came stealing towards her. Yet when it arrived, it proved to be the turning-point whence all her fortunes began to wane through a twilight of doubt and despondency to an ever deepening despair. Dan did not reappear on the day when he was expected. Stacey, in her ignorance, felt not a little aggrieved at the delay, although she was quite sure that the next morning would bring him. Twelve hours seem a vast void of time, when you have already begun to count your intervening minutes one by one. But after two or three more days had trailed immeasurably by, she would have been humbly thankful for an assurance that she would see him again within a twelvemonth. So quickly may we learn to abate our claims upon good fortune.

It wanted just a week of the wedding-day, when a man casually observed to Stacey's brother Matt, as they were hooding stooks below at Hilfirthy's, that he had seen Dan O'Beirne going on board the Stranraer steamer up at Larne, shortly before he had himself returned to Lisconnel. The poor little bride-elect put a brave face on the matter when the news was communicated to her, and said cheerfully that Dan would be apt to be writing to explain the way of it. But in truth her heart sank down and down, and she felt a miserable conviction that no letter was coming. Soon, too, she knew—though they said, "Shoo-whisht woman," and broke off when she came near—how the neighbours were often standing in knots and saying it had a bad appearance, his slipping off out of the country that fashion, without a word to anybody; it looked like as if he had a notion of running away from the match. The sight of those shawled heads bobbing together over her fate chilled Stacey with despair at times, and at others stung her with a wrathful pang, under which she could almost have found it in her heart to break up their conclave violently, accusing them to their faces of telling lies and talking blathers and nonsense. But she always stopped short of any such strong measures, quailing before her consciousness that her life was being overcast by a great black cloud, in the coming on of which this gossips' gabble seemed merely a trivial fringe of shadow; and the one discourtesy she used was to shrink away from all occasions of discourse, either sitting mute in a retired recess of the dark cabin-room, or roaming off into the bog, where the solitude and silence toned down the brightness of the clear careless skies and made it more endurable.

In this way it came about that the blue-vaulted forenoon, which by rights should have seen her conversion into Mrs. Daniel O'Beirne, was spent by Stacey in solitary forlornness, crouched among the sad-green furzes—" mindin' th' ould goat " was how she described her occupation to her neighbours—and that a few hours later found her standing up uncomforted on the ridge, turning mournful grey eyes listlessly towards the rose and daffodil sunset, before she crept home through the gloaming, lit by no brighter hope than the prospect of sleepily forgetting her troubles until to-morrow. Days such as this came to her in a sequence. For amid the mellow sunshine of the late-summer weather, which was transmuting the grain-fields to roughened gold, and staining the brier-leaves with bronze and crimson, and bringing out the dim purplish bloom on all the wild dark berries—dewberries and frawns and sloes—and even finishing off the little grey lichen-cups with red sealing-wax rims, Stacey's hopes were shrivelling up and withering away. She did not really try to blind herself, whatever mien she would fain have confronted her world with Each blank morning, and each cheerless evening, heard her paraphrase: " Even here I will put off my hope and keep it no longer for my flatterer ; " most piteous of vows, not oftener made than broken. After a few weeks had passed, she used to pray to her saints that she might not know of anybody going down to the Town, because she could not avoid the bitter moment of watching him return without letter or tidings.

Yet Stacey, sad as was her plight, should not monopolise our sympathy. Young Dan's unaccountable non-appearance flung a portentous shadow across his father's horizon. He was slower than the girl to take the alarm, his wider experience suggesting a larger variety of harmless contingencies; but when once fear got firm hold of him, it gripped him with a hardly less agonising rigour. If "anythin' misfortnit had took and happint" his big handsome son, the light of his eyes had been put out; but if the truth were that the lad had played a villain's trick on them, had given the lie to his hand-promise, and run off from them, leaving the girl to break her heart, why then old Dan was doubly bereft, both of trust and hope. Moreover, his distress was complicated by a feeling of compunction and responsibility towards Stacey and her family, which made the sight of them painful to him, and still forbade him to keep out of their way.

"'Tisn't the lad's own fau't, that's sartin," he said one late November day, sitting on an old potato-creel by Mrs. Doyne's fire. "If I know the differ between porther and potheen, he'd no more go for to do us a turn like that, except agin his will, than he'd reive the eyes out of his head. There's somethin' gone amiss wid him that we haven't heard tell of."

"True for you, Dan," said Mrs. Doyne, resignedly; "I put it on them ould steamboats meself; there's nothin' more dangerous. Sure the on'y time I iver made free wid one of them, a matter of twinty year back, away down at Lough Corrib, I came as nigh losin' me life as you could think—set me fut over the edge of the bit o' plank they'd laid down for the people to step on board by, and in the black wather I'd ha' been on'y poor Mick grabbed a-hould of me. And sure if Dan done such a thing, and he travellin' the deep says, let alone a lough, what chanst 'ud he have but goin' to the bottom? Or where's the use of the talk they keep of his sendin' word in letters, and he all the while lyin' dhrownded dead—the Lord have mercy on his sowl."

"Och then, goodness guide you, Mrs. Doyne, woman, but d'you think the lad's a born nathural that he's not got the wit to step the lenth of a bit of a gangway widout blundherin' overboard like an ould blind horse? Troth, it's a quare thing if a young man can't take a taste of divarsion for wunst in a way, but iverybody must settle to murdher him behind his back."

"Some of them do say 'twas that Maggie Farrelly he'd his mind set on all the while, and he's took off out of this liefer than contint himself wid any one else. It's no credit to him to sarve us that way. And the dacint lad he seemed, and the hape he thought of Stacey. Bedad, he wouldn't have given her for his pick of the stars out of the sky, if you were to believe him. I'd niver ha' supposed it of him, so I wouldn't."

"And it's great ould lies they were tellin', whoiver tould you that. Maggie Farrelly, bedad! Divil a hap'orth she was to him, let alone he isn't the *slieveen* to be playin' fast and loose wid your dacint little slip of a girl. It's little they've to do to be puttin' them bad stories on him, when he's overtook wid goodness can tell what ill-luck away from his own country."

"Musha, man alive, isn't that what I was sayin' a minit ago? Dhrownded he mayn't be for sartin, but there's plinty more manners of desthruction in it—plinty. Sure the strongest iver stepped might be took suddint, like a candle-light in a puff of win'—the saints purtect us all. There was Peter Molloy of Glenish, as fine a young man as you'd see, at Mass one Sunday, and waked the next. A beautiful corp he made, and so 'ud poor Dan— onless it *was* dhrownin' after all, and no layin' out to be done on him."

"Bad manners to it, woman, what talk have you of wakin' and burryin', and Maggie Farrelly? Cock her up! But it's true enough there do be girls will get round a man wid their slootherin', till he'll scarce know for a while what he's at; for a while just—it's past my belief that aught 'ud hould him long away from all of us here. I'm waitin' wid a job of plough-mendin' I have until he's back."

"Och well, it's yourself knows the warld, Dan, and tubbe sure he might aisy enough git into bad company in them parts, and he'd ha' nobody to advise him agin it, or purvint them makin' a fool of him, the young bosthoon, wid nary a thraneen of sinse in his head."

"Sinse is it? Bejabers Dan's got twyste the sinse of many a man double his age, and more to the back of that."

"It's liker, then, somethin' disprit's after happenin' him—the crathur. But 'deed, and if the end of it was to ha' been his comin' home married to another girl, as some of them's supposin', it's as black a day for us 'twould——"

Here Stacey, to whom this balancing of probabilities had been as soothing as alternate stabs of ice and flame, stole forth from her dusky corner, and slipped out at the door. Her mother, however, just saw her vanish, and said dismayed: "That was Stacey herself. Well now, I've a head, and so's a pin—I might ha' remimbered she came in afore you did. We'd a right to ha' held our tongues."

As Stacey emerged into the honey-coloured westering light, and began to saunter about aimlessly in the narrow grassy foot-tracks which threaded the shag of furze and heather on the slope behind her dwelling, she was descried by a group of neighbours who a little way off were watching Brian Kilfoyle cut scraws from a green-swarded bank for the repair of his roof. When she guessed their observation, she made a feint of looking for bogberries, which were, as every one knew, no longer in season, and moved slowly off out of sight.

"There goes poor Stacey Doyne," said Mrs. Brian, "moonin' along like some desolit ould crathur; it's a pity to see her."

"I just wish I had the regulatin' of that young rip Dan O'Beirne," said Mrs. Quigley; "I'd give him a goin' over he wouldn't be apt to forgit in one while."

"Sure how can we tell he's to blame?" said Mrs. Brian; "somethin's maybe gone agin' him. But any way, poor Stacey might as well put the thought of him out of her mind as soon as she can conthrive it. There's scarce a likeliness of his iver showin' his face agin in Lisconnel. We'll see that same wisp of cloud, that's after sailin' in behind the sun there, come sailin' back to us first —if you ask my opinion."

"Och Stacey—Stacey Doyne—*she* wouldn't be over-long troubled frettin' after him, if she had but the chanst of e'er another one handy," said Sally Sheridan, her words tumbling out thickly in a sudden spiteful flurry, as if they had been pent up unspoken for an irksome length of time. "She'll niver want for a sweetheart, if it depinds on herself, though maybe she doesn't find them so aisy to pick up. I'm thinkin' 'twas herself done most of the coortin' for young O'Beirne; *he* was in no great hurry over the matter—at all evints he was in a greater one to be shut of her."

"Just look here, me good girl," said the widow M'Gurk, "you've no call to be sayin' any such a thing now; none whatsomiver, even supposin' it was the truth you were tellin', instid of a black lie. Little Stacey Doyne's not the sort to be coortin' herself sweethearts; and she's no need, sorra a bit has she. For whativer may have come to him since, 'twas plain to be seen young Dan thought the warld hadn't her match, or anythin' fine enough for her in it."

"And let me tell you, Sally Sheridan," said Mrs. Rafferty, "that when a girl passes them kind of remarks, other people do be very apt to think she's judgin' accordin' to her own carryins on, and it gives her an oncommon onplisant appearance."

Miss Sally was in reality considerably disconcerted by the rebuke of her elders, who stood eyeing her severely from beneath their fluttering shawls, and who obviously had the sense of the company with them. However, she would not "let on" that she minded, and strolled away, snatching at the bushes as she passed, and humming a surly tune in a manner meant to indicate unconcern.

"But it's a pity, so it is, about Stacey," resumed Mrs. Brian, "you can see be the look of her that she's just frettin' herself to flitterjigs; and her poor mother was tellin' me yisterday that she'll scarce open her lips from mornin' till night, but sits mopin' in the corner, or sthreels off be herself on the bog. The poor woman's fairly disthracted wid onaisiness, and I don't wonder at it. They do say 'twas a disappointment of that sort gave Mad Bell's wits a turn; and if Stacey was to go like her, deminted poor ould body, bedad 'twould be a sorrowful sight, and fit to break the hearts of them that rared her—Sakes and patience, Jim! keep from under our feet, there's a good child; I was near waddlin' over you that time like an ould duck."

"Talkin' of Mad Bell," said Mrs. Rafferty, "she's away wid herself agin. Set off this mornin' afore it was light, so Big Anne tould me. Sez she to Anne: 'I'm afeard,' sez she, 'of them deep snow-dhrifts out there on the bog.' Goodness can tell what put snow in the crathur's head. 'Starvin' and perishin', starvin' and perishin',' sez she, ''twill be wid yous here this winter, and I'm away to the people where the ships is '—Galway belike. So off she wint."

"Well now, that's a bad hearin', mark my words," said Mrs. Quigley, looking scared; "Mad Bell and folk like her do have surprisin' notions about things, wheriver they git them. But there's no great signs that I can see of a hard winter comin' on us—would you say there was, Brian?"

"I dunno," said Brian, trimming the edges of a symmetrical smooth green sod; "I perceived a couple of saygulls flyin' inland this mornin', straight and steady—bad cess to them."

"But Brian," pursued Mrs. Quigley, dropping her voice, "have you heard any talk lately about *Thim Ones?* For since young Mick Ryan——"

"Och blathers," said Brian.

"Whisht, whisht then," said Mrs. Brian, turning away hastily, "the child's a-listenin'. Anyhow, I must be steppin' home."

"And I," said Mrs. Quigley. "Weary on it," she observed dejectedly, as they went down the road, "maybe Stacey's as well out of settin' up wid housekeepin' these times, if she knew but all. Starvin's bad enough for yourself, but when it comes to the childer—och wirra, that's starvin' wid heart-breakin' tacked on to the end of it."

Stacey, however, was as yet in no mood to take a philosophical view of the situation. She still carried her trouble in both hands, as we do with such things while they are new to us. Afterwards we generally stow them away in the pack which we keep on our shoulders, where they make their weight felt, it is true, but do not hinder us from going, more or less heavily, about our wonted avocations. And in mere course of time Stacey might so have disposed of hers, even if nothing had occurred to accelerate matters.

A day or two afterwards, she fell in with a crony of hers on one of her dismal bog-trottings. Jim Kilfoyle was a person who for some four years had been contemplating his world through a pair of very large and observant Irish-blue eyes, and drawing his own conclusions therefrom with an independence of thought which often gave the charm of originality to his theories. On the present occasion they had guided him to a spray of belated blackberries, which the vague November sunbeams had scarcely tinged even with the crudest red, but which he had no scruples about plucking in their rathest immaturity.

"Them berries are too green to be aitin', Jimmy," Stacey remonstrated mildly; but he curtly replied, "Here's two ones for yourself; and let me have a bit of food in paice." So she prudently gave up the point.

When he had swallowed, with inexplicable satisfaction, the last hard knob of sour seeds, he sat staring at Stacey for some time, and then said meditatively: "*I* don't think you look anyways so like Mad Bell, Stacey."

"Mercy be among us, Jim—like Mad Bell?" Stacey said, with a little laugh. At eighteen a pretty girl's vanity is perhaps the last peak to be submerged, and the first to reappear in any swelling tide of affliction, and a comparison between herself and the wizened little old cracked woman could not but strike her as grotesquely incongruous. "Sure what at all should ail me to be lookin' like Mad Bell, poor ould crathur?"

"Me mother sez so, then," said Jim, rather sternly for he suspected a disabling of his judgment in Stacey's laugh; "she and Mrs. Quigley yisterday, when you were above on the hill. Sthreelin' about like Mad Bell, they said you were, and fit to break iverybody's heart."

"Did they say—anythin' else, Jim?" said Stacey, with a catch in her voice, as if an icy gust had blown in her face and taken away her breath.

"Dunno," said Jim, and either could not or would not supply any further information.

But what he had stated made her feel hot and cold. Hitherto, so far as her dreary preoccupation allowed her to consider external affairs, she had believed that she was keeping her miseries strictly to herself, and betraying to nobody how her world had been turned into a wilderness. And now she abruptly learned that her conduct had led her neighbours to suppose her going daft, an intolerable revelation, against which all her pride rose up in arms. It found an auxiliary in the feeling of self-reproach roused by Jim's reference to the breaking of everybody's heart. For she knew very well that "everybody" in this connection could only mean her mother, towards whom she was conscious of having displayed during the past weeks a frank morosity and undisguised gloom. "As cross as an ould weasel, and as conthráry as anythin' you could give a name to," she called herself, in her awakening remorse. Under such circumstances, this demeanour, rightly interpreted, is often really tantamount to a friendly vote of confidence; yet it blackens in the retrospect when the memory, sensitised by the touch of conscience, is exposed to a new point of view. As Stacey sat silently beside the silent Jim, who had fallen to grubbing droves of scampering ants out of crevices in the bank with a little bit of twig, her thoughts turned upon troubles of which she was not the isolated victim; and when she presently got up and moved away, she said to herself:

"I'll slip home and be diggin' the pitaties for dinner." The resolution sounds scarcely heroic, yet it nevertheless marks the place where Stacey, so to speak, faced about. A retreat in some disorder had been converted into a rally.

As if in confirmation of the saying that fortune favours the brave, Stacey soon happened upon a small scrap of comfort, which, flimsy as was its material, sometimes stood her in good stead. On that same afternoon, her half-instinctive groping about among her scanty resources for some object of distraction, ended in a determination to step out and ask Peg Sheridan for the loan of a skein of yarn, with which she might set herself up a piece of knitting. "Peg's been oncommon good-natured," she reflected; "she'll let me have it in a minit, if she's got e'er a thread." But on her way to the Sheridans, Stacey was overtaken by old Ody Rafferty, who quitted his digging to shout that he hadn't seen her for a month of Sundays, and came shuffling down the potato-drill with uncludible nimbleness to intercept her at the dyke. She could not, without marked incivility, avoid stopping to speak, and when they had duly said, "How's yourself this long while?" and, "Finely, glory be to goodness," Ody prevented her from passing on by catching a corner of her shawl.

"Stacey, me child, listen now to me," he said; "I was wantin' to tell you you've no call to be discouraged anyways about young Dan not comin' home."

Stacey listened submissively. She was by this time acquainted with most of her neighbours' several theories as to her sweetheart's defection, and they were not on the whole consolatory.

"I'll tell you the way of it, Stacey," he said, "he's just took and enlisted. That's what he's after doin', and don't believe any one that sez anythin' differint. Sure, I've a right to know what I'm talkin' about, considerin' I've been well acquainted wid the lad from the time he was three feet high—that stands six-fut-two this day in his stockin' feet. It's many the mile we've thramped togither, himself, and meself, and misfortnit poor Jinny, and I know as well as I know me own name that he'd a great notion of soldierin'. Troth, I could ha' tould you that much iver since one day I saw him standin' lookin' after a milithry band that went by us down at Kilmacrone. And be the powers of smoke, he'll make a grand dragoon, Dan will; proud any regiment might be to git a hould of him. 'Twould do one's heart good to see him in his uniform—and so we will one of these fine days, for you may depind he's just schemin' to give us a quare ould surprise wid marchin' in on us in all his ilegance; and that's the raison why's he's niver said a word—just to take us unbeknownst. Not but what it may be a while first. I shouldn't wonder if Dan was apt to wait till he's got a bit of promotion. The idee I have in me own mind is that he'll likely put it off till he's riz to be a colour-seargint"—I fancy that Ody's own mind supposed this officer to derive his title from the peculiar gorgeousness of his accoutrements—"and then he'll come back a sight to behould, he that wint off wid the daylight shinin' thro' the ould coat was on him like a fire blinkin' behind a gapped dyke. Och Stacey, it's the proud girl you'll be that day, jewel; that set up, you'll scarce have a word for one of the rest of us."

"I'm sure I niver thought to mind him bein' raggetty like," said Stacey piteously. "And how'd he come home, seargint or no, if they're maybe sendin' him off to be kilt in the wars?"

"Is it kilt? Divil a much! Why, for one thing, I dunna believe there's e'er a war in it now, good or bad. I was spellin' over an ould *Cork 'Xaminer* a couple of days ago, and sorra a sign of a war could I see in it at all, no more than if the warld had took to wool-windin'. And another thing is, accordin' to what I'm informed, the throops these times don't iver get fightin' rightly at all, but just slinge about aisy miles off aich other, and let fly an odd cannon-ball or so now and agin to pacify whoiver it was sent them out. So it's a comical thing if an infant child, let alone a grown man, couldn't stand clare of that much widout puttin' himself greatly about. I tell you you needn't be vexin' your mind, Stacey, for as sure as me sowl's in me body it's enlisted Dan is, and steppin' home to Lisconnel he'll be afore we're any of us much oulder. He's the lad that 'ud niver go for to disremimber the ould people, and the ould place, let alone his bit of a *colleen dhu*—not if he was to become Head Commander-in-Gineral by land and say."

Ody spoke with sincere conviction, and a wonted authoritativeness which did not fail to impress Stacey, and through many succeeding days she clung to the colour-sergeant hypothesis as desperately as if it had been a life-buoy instead of a straw. In the long dark evenings, when it was too cold to lie down away from the fire on the puddly floor, and in the bleak mornings, when life waking up found Nought the answer persistently elicited by computations of happiness in prospect—a result which eighteen years old is prone to regard as a *reductio ad impossibile*—Stacey sometimes shut out intrusive despairs with the help of Ody's glowing picture. Only it invariably happened that the martial figure, flaring and glittering along the bog-road, turned, before he came very near, into just Dan himself in his old scarecrow tatters, without any splendour or brilliancy at all. She had much need, in truth, of whatever cheering figments either faith or fancy could frame. For this winter was a pitiless season to Lisconnel and its inhabitants.

One December night they all shivered sorely in their lairs of heather and rags, as if the breath of a bitter frost were abroad. Still, in the morning no traces of such were visible, unless you noticed that the lingering brier and bracken leaves seemed suddenly to have been dipped in fierily vivid scarlet and orange. But when the potatoes for the next meal were gathered, faces lengthened and heads shook; for experienced eyes at once recognised signs of a "frost-blighting" that must entail a serious shrinkage of estimated supplies. And soon after that they began to draw omens from the flights of birds, flocks, mainly, of seagulls small and great, who came swooping over the mirk of the bog, lighting on it in patches of foam, scattered momently in a flickering of white wings as they fled on further inland. Herons, too, passed, heavily and gloomily flapping and croaking; and long trains of wild duck, scudding by like trails of smoke that knew where it was going, till they dwindled into blurred pencil-marks on the horizon

All these, if they did not exactly belong to "the nation of uniortunate and fatal birds," were watched coming and going by foreboding eyes, as the harbingers of "powerful severe weather when they do be that plinty."

And, sure enough, before Christmas there was deep snow. It came wavering across the bogland on a north-west wind, and lay strewn at first in handfuls, and then in armfuls, till at last a huge lead-coloured cloud appeared to shatter itself sheer over Lisconnel—" Like as if," to quote Pat Ryan, "you were crumblin' a soft clod of clay between your two hands;" and thenceforward all was one blank of white, only broken here and there by the black mouth of a bog-hole. Even these filled eventually, as the water in them froze hard, and made of each a secret resting-place for the whirling drifts, pitfalls into one of which the Quigley's fawn-coloured goat floundered down, poor wretch, to her smothering death. For the snow was accompanied by such a biting frost as seldom grips Lisconnel, and the tiny dry flakes and granules seemed to be ground fine and driven in tangible mists of stinging dust on the wide-wailing storm.

"It's a good chanst we're gettin' to understand the sayin':

"'When you see the snow like salt and male,
Your food and fire'll be apt to fail,'"

Brian Kilfoyle said one day, ruefully kicking at a glittering powdery drift, which had sifted under the Doyne's rickety door into their house, where he was talking to Stacey and her mother. Brian, who is normally a big burly man, at that time had assumed, in common with his neighbours, the aspect of an incomplete structure, a framework with much filling out left to do. "It's siven weeks lyin' on us now sin' Christmas, and here's Candlemas wid nary a sign of a change yit. But I'm glad to see you houldin' up so well agin it, ma'am."

"Och, indeed I'm keepin' iligant and grand, thank God," said Mrs. Doyne, nervously fingering the largest hole in her frayed-out apron. "But as for Stacey there, the crathur, her face this minit isn't the breadth of the palm o' me hand; the two eyes of her'll prisintly be runnin' into one."

Stacey shrank further into the background at the sound of her own name, and Brian Kilfoyle said: "Ah, sure young things like her do be aisy perished—aye, and the ould people too. There's me poor mother, she and little Jim, since the bad turn he took a while ago, they don't seem to have an atom of warmth left in them. Scarce a wink they sleep of a night wid the could, though we do give them ivery rag we can conthrive. Our hearts are fairly broke wid them; for me mother, if we don't mind her, will be slippin' the wisp of an ould cloak off her on to one of the childer, and gittin' her death ; and that Jim does be creepin' from one to the other like a lost dog at a fair, thryin' for a taste of heat somewheres, the misfortnit little spalpeen ; its hands grabbin' you do be just dabs of ice. But divil a thraneen more have we got to put on them."

There was a painful pause, and then Mrs. Doyne said, apologetically : " I wish to goodness gracious, Brian, I could offer you the loan of e'er an ould wrap, but indeed it's hard set we are, man, to keep the life from freezin' stiff in ourselves these times, wid the most we've got."

"Tubbe sure, tubbe sure, ma'am," Brian said, in hurried deprecation, " how would you ? Sure we must all shift for ourselves the best way we can, and we'll do right enough wunst this blamed black frost quits a hould."

Brian had now carried out the purpose of his call, but he could not betray the fact by immediate departure, so he lingered gossiping in the doorway.

" Big Anne's sleepin' up at Widdy M'Gurk's these couple of nights back, did you hear tell ? " he began. " She got that scared and lonesome there be herself she couldn't abide it."

For Mad Bell was, as we know, absent, and the Dummy had been some years dead.

"So they were sayin'," said Mrs. Doyne. "But look-a, Brian"—lowering her voice solemnly—"div you know was there—anythin' special frightened her?"

"Well, yis," he answered, in a reluctant sort of mumble, "a fut goin' up and down along be her door, and nobody on the road; and somethin' that shook the latch and let a keen, and niver a breath of win' stirrin'. Lastewise that's the story she has. But just you tell me how many nights in the year there is widout a waft of win' goin' thro' it; and as for them bastes of goats, times and agin I've mistook a one of them pattin' by for somethin' in brogues. Howsome'er, what fairly tirrified her was a voice that kep' callin' 'Anne, Big Anne,' imitatin' first one neighbour, and then another, and diff'rint in a manner from them all. She sez 'twas such hijeous clare moonlight she dursn't look out, and she lay in a could thrimble till the mornin', listenin' to a tappin' on the window—she'd stopped up the pane wid her ould saucepan-lid for 'fraid she might see somethin'. That was rattlin' belike."

"Saints shield us around," said Mrs. Doyne, crossing herself, "we'd be well off if there was nothin' worse than saucepans rattlin'. You've heard tell what happint young Mick Ryan about Holy Eve, when he'd a crib set for snipe be the river?"

Brian only said, "Aye, aye," uninvitingly, but she could not forego the recital:

"Just liftin' the basket he was, when he looked up, and if there wasn't *Wan of Thim* standin' on the opposite bank right fornint him, wid on'y the flow of the bit of sthrame between them—and *the Other* comin' jiggin' along over the strip of field, not a stone's throw off. Troth, poor Mick thought he couldn't git his heels out of it fast enough. I wonder he didn't lose his wits for good. When he fetched home, his people thought he was blind drunk—Och mercy, what at all's yon out there, Brian?" she interrupted herself, suddenly clutching him by the arm, and pointing through the open door. Far out upon the blanched waste something there was, moving dimly in the thickened light of the gloaming, but whether the form of man or beast, or of neither, could not be told. Brian, without speaking, went a step outside, and seemed to measure the distance which intervened between his own door and the place where he stood.

"It's just merely one of the goats trapesin' around," he said.

Then he made a plunge, and rushed towards his cabin across the clogging snow, stumbling and tripping in a headlong haste, for which there was nothing apparent to account. Mrs. Doyne banged and bolted the door behind him; and when, long after·

wards, her two sons came home, they were obliged to kick and shake it for some time, with much strong language, uttered in unmistakably familiar tones, before courage enough was screwed up inside to give them admission.

On the next morning, Mrs. Doyne, coming in with an icicle-fringed bucket, sustained another shock of a different kind. Stacey was sitting with folds of brown stuff spread about her, and with needle and thread in hand. It was the material got for her wedding-gown, cut out by Biddy Ryan, who is "quare and cute" about such things, and partially sewn together by Stacey's mother, before the day when the girl had passionately implored that it might be put away out of her sight, since when it had lain hidden underneath the dresser.

"I was considerin' the skirt would make a little sort o' frock like for the Kilfoyles' Jim," Stacey said in explanation. "'Tis bad to be thinkin' of the bit of an imp perishin' all night. Then the lenth of grey holland 'ud make a petticoat might help to keep the life in ould Mrs. Kilfoyle; I'd be sorry anythin' took her."—The old woman had soothed Stacey's spirit by expressing confidence in the honesty of Dan.—"And there'll be enough wincey left yit to ready up a body for your ugly ould self."

"Och honey, but supposin' you might be wantin'

it one of these days after all?" said Mrs. Doyne unable to refrain from a protest against this implied abandonment of hope.

"Niver a want I'll want it," said Stacey. "He's dead and gone, mother jewel. 'Tis a sin to lave it lyin' up; there's a beautiful warmth in it. And I've set me mind on it oncommon."

So Mrs. Doyne assented, as she would to most things upon which Stacey with her great wistful eyes had set her mind; this acquiescence, however, not barring sundry bitter thoughts of a Dan hypothetically in the land of the living.

Stacey sewed hard all day, with horrible gobble-stitches it must be owned, for her education had been sadly neglected in many of its branches; besides which, the cold would scarcely let her hold the needle. By the time the daylight failed, she had finished two very quaint garments, whose cut would not bear criticism, but warm and stout of fabric. She felt impatient to convey them to the Kilfoyles; yet as she looked out over the gleaming snow, which had drawn all the light down out of the blank sky, some uncanny thoughts came before her mind so vividly that she shrank from traversing even those few roods of ground alone, and she determined to wait until her brothers came in. But as the evening wore on, and they did not arrive, she grew more and more fidgety,

It would be a cruel pity to let Jim freeze through another whole night; his small cold hands seemed to keep dragging her towards the door; and at last she said to herself that she would chance it: maybe there wasn't a word of truth in them quare stories all the while; *she'd* niver seen aught. Watching her time, therefore, she stole out unobserved with her bundle into the moonlight.

She wished it had not been so bright. Just to run on blindly through dark shadows, which kept discreetly hidden whatever unchancy objects they might hold, would have seemed easier than to face that broad white glare, where anything dreadful would be seen so very plainly. The rush was made, however, without incident; and then Stacey sped out of the Kilfoyles' cabin almost as precipitately as she had sped into it, running away from the bewildered gratitude of its inhabitants, and the importunate memories and contrasts which this final disposition of her wedding gear did not fail to arouse.

But when she had gone only a few paces from their door, a sudden panic seized her. She was compelled by a sort of irresistible fascination to look fearfully round over the wilds that lay stark about and about her, as solitary as the unfathomed blue-black deeps, with their frost-burnished full moon and light-drowned star-flecks. Wafts of wind came murmuring from the far distance, here and there sweeping up a whirl of powdery flakes, as if some one lifted a corner of the great white sheet and let it fall again in a rumpled fold. The wind, of course, was full of sighs and voices, and shadows wavered and flitted on the snow. How could she tell what they might be? Suppose she should meet that strange little crying child, whom people said sometimes ran after them when they were late abroad on the bog? Or the limping old woman, who laughs in your face as she goes by? Terror whirled through Stacey's thoughts like an autumn gust among a drift of fallen leaves. She began to dart along as fast as the deep snow, a nightmare-like drag, would permit, and she kept her eyes fixed desperately on the track she trod in. Quite near her own door, however, she had to slacken her pace, because across her path stretched two furrow-shaped snow-drifts, into whose ungauged depths she dared not plunge her bare foot. And as she paused a moment irresolute, a voice close by spoke abruptly. "You'll have to git over them," it said, "in standin' leps, as the Divil wint thro' Athlone." Stacey did not scream or fly, for she knew the voice, and it was one which would have reassured her in the teeth of a North American blizzard, or the heart of a West Indian cyclone "So it's yourself, Dan," she said.

Dan O'Beirne it was, a tall, gaunt, ragged figure, standing up blackly just beyond the sharp-cut shadow of the Doynes' cabin wall. "Aye, 'tis so," he said, with an anxious hurry in his manner. "And are you thinking intirely too bad of me, Stacey, that I sted away so long? And you not hearin' a word, I'm tould, 'xcipt the letter I sint be Paddy Loughlin, the sthookawn, that you niver got. Meself it is, sure enough, and pounds and pounds, and somethin' I stopped to get you up at Larne—on'y—there's the use of one hand mostly disthroyed on me, and I dunno, tellin' you the truth, if I'll iver walk any better than a trifle lame wid me left fut—just a trifle. Och, but, Stacey *asthore*, maybe you'd liefer have nought to say to such an ould bosthoon of misery?"

"Sure it's all one," said Stacey, "why you sted away, since it's home you are agin; and the sorra a much I'd be mindin' if you hadn't a hand or a fut left on you at all, at all." A speech whereof the first clause sounds rather poor-spirited, and the last distinctly unfeeling; but to which Dan took no exception.

He could give a more detailed account of himself, however, to less incurious friends, whom he told how, on finishing his engagement at the peat-factory, a temptingly lucrative job had lured him over the straits to Scotland, whence he intended to

return about Holy Eve, which change of plan he
announced in a letter home, confided to one Paddy
Loughlin, who proved an unreliable messenger. The
truth is that Paddy "cliver and clane" forgot his
friend's letter in his own bustle about transmitting
his earnings home in postal orders, and getting
himself shipped back as a pauper to the most con-
veniently-situated Union—a thrifty, if not strictly
legitimate, mode of travelling occasionally adopted
by itinerant harvest-men. How, just before he
should have started for home, he met with a bad
accident while helping to rescue the factory foreman's son out of a whirl of jag-toothed wheels and
hissing bands, "like so many spider's webs all set
a-goin' by the Divil," and had lain for a couple of
months crippled in hospital, whence he had sent
no word, "lest they'd be fretted thinkin' he was
took for death away from them all."

"Oncommon kind people," ran his account of
his experiences there, "and iverythin' done as agreeable as they could conthrive, barrin' that them
doctors would be lookin' in of a mornin' and sayin',
'That leg had a right to come off to-morra,' or
'He'll lose them two fingers, anyway,' as aisy and
plisant as if the flesh wasn't creepin' on your bones
to hear them. But sure they were intindin' no harm ;
it's the nature of them to keep choppin' and sawin'.
The on'y wonder is that any one gits out of a place

where they do be plinty, wid enough of his body left him to hould his sowl in." Then how, recovering, unmulct after all of limb, he had straightway repaired home, bringing with him the "pounds and pounds" presented to him by the grateful foreman, a suit of clothes much too good to think of wearing, and the promise of permanent employment at Sterry and Lawson's, whenever he chose to return.

Even so, Dan's home-coming could not be compared for external brilliancy with that of the colour-sergeant. Indeed, after the first raptures of restoration had subsided, the elder Dan cast many a regretful glance at the halting gait and sling-suspended arm of his tall son; while Ody Rafferty sought to slur over the refutation of his own conjectures by insisting on the fact that, if the lad *had* took off to the most outrageous wars iver was, he'd more likely than not have come out of them with less destruction done on him than might be perceived now. Young Dan's native air seemed, however, to possess very salubrious qualities; and before he had been three weeks at home, his step began to regain its firmness, and strength and suppleness returned to his limp wrist and stiffened fingers. His cure was practically complete by the time that the black frost had broken, and the snow had vanished off the bog, leaving only its wraith on the frail-blossomed sloe-bushes, and the wedding-day had come.

I met the bridal-party proceeding towards the Town on Farmer Hilfirthy's loaned jaunting-car, and it struck me that I had never seen so many people at once on any vehicle. I caught a glimpse of Jim Kilfoyle in a queer brown frock sitting on the well, and just as they passed he was saying sternly: " I' clare, Biddy Sheridan, if you don't lave houldin' me on, I'll let the greatest ould yell you iver heard, and terrify the horse."

This was a morning in Easter week, and Lady Day in Spring too—a coincidence which led the widow M'Gurk to observe that you might meet as good fortune marrying on one Lady Day as another: a happy-go-lucky sentiment which Lisconnel appears disposed to adopt as a piece of local proverbial philosophy.

CHAPTER IX.

BACKWARDS AND FORWARDS.

SHOULD it be concluded from facts related in the foregoing chapters that truth for truth's sake is rather at a discount in Lisconnel, I can scarcely gainsay the inference. If "lettin' on," "romancing a bit," and "just humbuggin'," with a little blarneying and sluthering thrown in, are over-straitly judged, we shall be found in a parlous state. But there is one point on which the veracity of its inhabitants, like that of many other people similarly situated, seems exposed to less warrantable suspicion. It is a commonly received opinion that the dwellers in any remote and lonely district are largely responsible for whatever growths of ghostly legend may flourish there. These, although they do not perhaps spring directly from anybody's invention, are, it is held, sedulously fostered and cultivated, and handed down with additions and improvements from generation to generation, who take a sort of pride and pleasure in them. We have all heard how the peasants gather round their hearths on eerie winter evenings, and beguile the time with the recital of marrow-freezing ghost stories, to which they contribute, at any rate, wilfully credulous minds.

No doubt this custom does really exist in some places; but I can confidently assert that it is not to be found in Lisconnel, and, failing personal observation, I should venture to think its general prevalence antecedently improbable. People who live their li es in solitary places of the earth, under a rigorous enforcement of all the penalties of Adam, are little likely to hanker after the introduction of any supernatural crooks into their lot; to voluntarily fill the wild blasts wailing round their poor hovels with unearthly shrieks and lamentations, that bid them spend their long night imagining some fear, or beset their fields with prowling phantoms, that cause them on their lonely road to "walk in doubt and dread." In Lisconnel, certainly, there is none of this *vult decipi*. On the contrary, such things are, if accepted at all, accepted under protest. There is a marked tendency to resist the admission of spectres to the hamlet and its purlieus, and to resent any obstinate assertion of their presence. Johnny Ryan, for instance, will fight you any day—supposing you a possible combatant—to uphold his contention that he "niver saw or heard aught on the bogland quarer than it might be an ould white goat glimmerin' in a strake of moonlight, or a saygull lettin' a screech goin' by." And considerable ingenuity is expended in euhemerising uncanny personages, and explaining away mysterious appearances. How much of whatever belief in spectral hauntings has survived these critical methods may be the unconscious work of imagination, on which opposition sometimes acts as a stimulus, is of course a different question.

You have seen already some traces of its survival; and, indeed, if you consult a certain section of the community, you will learn facts which you would, if I am not mistaken, be glad to disprove, did you happen to live in Lisconnel. You will hear not only of fearsome wanderers met a-field, but of strange forms found cowering by the hearth at home, and stealing away to lurk in dusky nooks, whence no one dares more than surmise their ultimate withdrawal. Of a shadow lying black all day across the threshold, with nothing visible to cast it, but falling ice-cold upon whomsoever makes bold to step over it. Of a lame old woman, who comes tapping at your door, it may be in the broad noonlight—a harmless-seeming old creature you think, until she looks into your eyes and laughs a laugh you will not soon forget the sound of. All the lore, in short, connected with those beings whom Lisconnel terms collectively, more or less under its breath, *Thim Wans.*

The origin of these visitations now lies obscured in the history of such old unhappy things, that it has come to be narrated in more various ways than I can here recount. But one of our local tragedies, said to be still terribly commemorated, did actually occur within the recollection of anybody who has had the sorrowful fortune to live through the great Famine year; that is, some half-century since. It was down at Classon's Boreen, a few miles along the road towards the Town, where a skeleton cabin stands to-day, that a man, driven distraught with the famine-fever, barred himself and three or four small children into their room, while the mother went in quest of food. And when she returned with some bread at nightfall, through the snow, the poor wretch would not open to her. So all night she beat on the door, and called to her crying children; and the next day the whole family were found cold and dead, the father and children in the cabin, and the mother outside, half-buried in a drift heaped against the wall, her loaf untouched, and in her hand the stone with which she had been battering the door. The cabin has been ever since deserted, and its doorway is a ruinous gap. Yet still on many a night, they say, this miserable woman may be seen standing by it, wringing her hands and buffeting the empty air. If you can take to your heels and fly before you have beheld anything more, you will have met with nothing worse than a fright. But if she turns and beckons you to come and help her, you could be given no surer warning of black troubles in store.

This was just what did befall Brian Kilfoyle one spring evening not long after young Dan's wedding, on his dusky way home from O'Beirne's forge with a mended *loy*. Brian's belief in ghostly manifestations is as a rule waveringly reluctant, and he would probably soon have reasoned himself into a conviction that he was only "after mistakin' somethin' in the darkness of the light," had not his mood been already downcast and foreboding, on account of his mother's failing health. For the past winter had proved a crucial test to all Lisconnel's feeble folk, and few of them had struggled through it unscathed. Some of them, indeed, had come out on the wrong, or at any rate, the *other* side. The Pat Ryans had lost their youngest twin child, which was still of a size to be called by the neighbours indifferently "Joe" and "Molly," and which used to trot a long way after either of its parents when it saw them going anywhere. Old Mick Ryan, too, had died at the end of several days' lethargy, so deep that it was impenetrable by even the tobacco, to purchase which his daughter, elderly Biddy, ran into debt, besides nearly walking herself off her legs in a forced march to the Town and back. Under these circumstances Brian was in the humour to take quick alarm at his mother's weakness and flagging spirits, and now his impression that the dark figure standing in the ruined doorway had turned round and beckoned to him through the twilight, put a finishing touch to his uneasiness. So much so that he resolved upon the extreme measure of seeking qualified medical advice, and to that end obtained a "red ticket" from Father Rooney.

Whereupon to Lisconnel came, Dr. Ward being on leave, a youthful *locum tenens*, whose amiable qualities created a favourable impression, dashed with a doubt that such a slip of a lad could have had " e'er a scrumption of experience " to authorise his opinions. His report upon his patient was to the effect that he could see little amiss with her.

" Sure it's active and robustuous enough your mother seems to be for a body of her time of life " —he was thus represented as expressing himself by Mrs. Brian—" but in coorse it stands to raison she isn't altogether as young as she was a while ago." Not having a turn for obvious pleasantries, he had given up adding in such cases : " She ought to have plenty of strengthening food."

"And 'Goodness guide you, sir,' sez I to him 'sure she wasn't *that* afore iver you were born or thought of,' sez I," continued Mrs. Brian, who appeared somewhat illogically to consider this repartee a refutation of the doctor's cautiously worded statement. Her husband, on the other hand, felt by no means disposed to cavil at the verdict, which relieved his fears so happily, that when he escorted the young man to his horse, he observed with strong emphasis, "It's rael *delightful* weather we're gettin' now, your honour," although the bog was just then livid with low-creeping flocks of pale mist, and the day had been as consistently dismal and lack-lustre a one as ever spent its drizzling hours in what we call neither raining nor letting it alone.

The last Saturday in the following June was a shining contrast. A morning risen behind lattices of fretted snow-sheen, which melted, with ever-widening interspaces, far up and away into faint lines and filmy streaks like the clouding on an agate, until, while the greensward underfoot was yet all beaded with prisms of dew, the lapis lazuli cup overhead curved down without a fleck from brim to brim. It was to be rather an eventful day for Lisconnel, by reason of a fair held in the Town, at which several of the neighbours proposed to sell their pigs and poultry. Lisconnel always sells its

few pigs about this season, not because they are
fat, but because the need of a little ready money
becomes coercive in the month before potato-
digging. The place does not, I must admit, excel
in swine, a fact hardly to be marvelled at, when
one considers how much plain living is perforce
practised by the animals during their sojourn
among us. Even if it is accompanied by the corre-
sponding high thinking, which must remain a
matter of conjecture, that does not influence market
prices. Seldom, in the case of a Lisconnel pig,
will any amount of hopeful prodding and poking
establish in its owner's mind a comfortable assurance of good condition ; though a refractory beast,
who has to be hauled shrieking out of a hole, or
lifted over a dyke, is conventionally described as
" the weight of any ten, begorrah." Yet, however
humble our own opinion of our wares may be, it is
trying to find the same confirmed for us, sarcastically, by other people. We do not like to be
greeted after a long trudge by inquiries such as :
" Wasn't it maybe a coorsin'-match you were intindin' to show them at all the while ? " or, " Might you
iver ha' happint to take notice that in some places
the pigs do have a fashion of wearin' their bones
the wrong side o' their skins?" or, "What at all
do you be feedin' the bastes on up at Lisconnel?
Ould scythe-blades, belike? or is it an odd taste of

a slim-handled hay-rake?" These questions have before now been settled, temporarily, with the help of fists and blackthorns.

The market folk set off betimes this morning, and as many of their neighbours were out on the bog cutting turf, the place grew very quiet, when once the squealing and squawking, which attended their progress, had died distantly away. It felt like a Sunday to the stayers at home, and it was partly this, and partly the glorious weather that brought them together in a session on an undulating bank of fine sward interspersed with boulders set flat in heathery rims, a favourite holiday lounging place, not far from the Kilfoyles' cabin. Old Mrs. Kilfoyle was among them, brisker again in response to the call of June, but physically almost extinguished under the folds of her daughter-in-law's ample blue cloak, with which her winter's indisposition had been made a long-sought pretext for investing her, much against her will. Even Peter Sheridan made a shift to hobble out of doors, not leaving behind him his rheumatics—" and bad scran to them "—whose companionship is, however, least obtrusive, when he can sit quiet in the warm clasp of the sun.

Its beams came long and slanting still, when the two last of the party bound for the fair were almost ready to start—the widow M'Gurk and Brian

Kilfoyle. Brian was going as a buyer, not a seller, having disposed of his pig a week ago, when, finding that small pigs went "cruel dear," he deferred the purchase of its successor in hopes to getting a better bargain later on. But the widow had on hands both her pig, and a clocking hen, with which, a clutch of eggs being unattainable, she had regretfully resolved to part. Brian had waited to assist her in the transportion of this live stock; but the hen, with a perverse prescience characteristic of her race, had at the last moment taken ungainly flight, and was now being pursued by himself and all the children out of arms. Meanwhile, Mrs. M'Gurk ready equipped for her journey, paused by the wayside group with her lean pig in a string.

"We'd do right to lave that ould rogue of a hin behind us," she said uneasily, while her beast fell to grazing industriously, as if bent upon adding at least a shilling to his market value, "she'll only be delayin' the man and spoilin' of his chances."

"Och, they'll grab her prisintly, no fear; she can't keep that work up very long, try her best," said old Mrs. Kilfoyle, placidly listening to the receding sounds of the pursuit. "Sit you down, Mrs. M'Gurk, ma'am, and be takin' the weight off of your feet while you can. I hope you'll have good luck with that crathur there; he seems to be a tidy level little baste."

"I wish I may do as well as Brian himself done last day wid his," said the widow. "'Twas a grand price entirely he got out of thim, and if he can pick up a weeny one any ways raisonable, he'll be right enough, plase God. And we've a notion what else he'll be bringin' home wid him this evenin', over and above, haven't we now, Mrs. Ryan?" she added, glancing at Mrs. Kilfoyle, and winking with weather-beaten archness.

"Troth have we," said Judy Ryan, "the same sort of notion I've got of what Mr. Corr does be weighin' out of a yaller-papered box wid black scrawms to it, and charges eightpince the quarther-poun' for, and blows open a purple bag to put it in—and then if your kettle's boilin', and your water's not smoked, 'twill be yourself's to blame if you haven't an iligant cup of tay." Judy was happily unconscious that the end of her enigma had escaped rather prematurely from its subtle enfoldures.

"Aye, aye," said the little old woman, looking round her from friendly face to face in a pleased flutter, "Brian does be very good." And everybody smiled and winked and nodded approval, being fully in the secret of Brian's intentions.

Everybody except Biddy Sheridan, who looked suddenly disconsolate, as if at a pang of jarred memory, where she sat peeling flakes of shaggy grey lichen off a sun-warmed stone. "Me brother

Mick,' she said, in a semi-soliloquising murmur, "he'd very belike ha' been thinkin' of bringin' home a bit of baccy this night wid him, too, if there was e'er a one left to set store by it. Mick niver begrudged aught he could do for his ould father, I'll say that for him. It wasn't in him—not when he had his own way." There was just a tinge of resentment in the last words.

"And bedad now, Biddy"—her sister-in-law's tone was undisguisedly deprecating—"bedad now, woman alive, nobody could lay it agin us that we either of us iver begrudged the poor ould man— God be good to him—bit or sup, or any trifle of warmth or comfort we had the givin' of. I'm not goin' for to deny but that I might be a bit put past me patience—goodness forgive me—now and agin, when times was bad, to see his ould pipe puff-puffin. 'Twas in a way like throwin' the childer's scrap of food behind the fire."

"Accordin' to my considerin'," Mrs. Kilfoyle's falsetto flute-piping interposed before Biddy could reply, "that baccy's a humbuggin' kind of ould stuff. Sure that's plain on the face of it, for excipt it was lettin' on to be somethin' diff'rint from itself, who'd give a brass farthin' for the likes of it? A little black-lookin' lump you've as much botheration gittin' a smoulder of red out of as if it was a wet sod of turf, and risin' such a smell—faix you might think they'd a cart-load of pratie-haulms burnin' in the pipe-bowl; on'y I'd a dale liefer have that for a scent—och, but I remimber it in the fields at home. But the fact of the matter is, smokin's just a notion the crathurs have; when they git taken up wid it, 'tis the same to them as a paiceable sort of drunkness, and puts the thought of the throubles they're in the middle of out of their heads. Many's the time I'd think to meself, Biddy, when I'd see your poor father sittin' inside there, wid his feet in a puddle of rain, and the could win' freezin' mad, and he lookin' fit to drop, and he contintin' himself all the while wid the ould pipe that was near shakin' out of his hand, the crathur— many's the time I'd be thinkin' 'tis a poor case to ha' nothin' between yourself and all the Divil's work about you better than a few streels of baccy-smoke. Och, girl dear, we've no call to go wish any one back agin widin his reach, that's after givin' him the slip for good and all, and needn't be schamin' ways to disremimber himself and his tormintin' thricks."

"That's the truth, ma'am," said Peter Sheridan, hoarsely, at her elbow.

"I dunno, then," said Mrs. M'Gurk, who stood fronting the assembly, with her elongated shadow grotesquely deflected against the sunny bank, and who evidently entered her protest from a sense of duty, "I dunno how you're rightified in makin' sure you'll be shut of the Divil as soon as you quit out of this, be any manner of manes. Bedad it may be quite the other way. My opinion of him is, you niver can tell where he'll have you, dead or alive. For anythin' we know he might be doin' as much agin us one place as the other, or maybe more, and bad luck to him."

"Well, it's clare enough to me," said Mrs. Kilfoyle, "and the way I look at it is this. There's little misdoubtin' that the Divil's plinty of sinse, howiver he come by it, and knows what he's about, God forgive him, as well as you or me. And he wouldn't be disthressin' himself the way he is to keep annoyin' people, if he didn't perceive that it was here he's gettin his best chanst of doin' mischief on us, and nowhere else. He wouldn't give himself that much throuble, you may depind, if he thought he'd have us readier to his hand, merely be waitin' till the breath was out of one's body—not he; he's too cute. For look at the carryins on of him; look at the conthrivances he has, and the invintions. Sure there's nothin', big or little, he wouldn't be for meddlin' in, though it might be a matter you'd niver think he'd need to consarn himself wid, 'xcipt he was fairly dhruv to it. And even so, he hasn't it all his own way; for wheniver his Betters have the time, now and agin, to be keepin' an eye on him, he's bound to quit interferin', and iverythin' goes plisant enough, and no thanks to him. Aye bedad, he gits a disappointment of an odd while, like any cne else in this world ; and, mark my words, he wouldn't be spendin' so much of his days in it, if there was e'er another place he could regulate more to his mind."

"Onless 'twas for divarsion like," suggested Judy Ryan, "the same way that Quality do come sthravadin' on the bog wid their guns, and wadin' up to their knees in the rivers, after the bits of birds and fish, and they wid more than they can ait at home all the while, if it was that that ailed them."

"Divarsion? why, woman dear, in coorse it's divarsion to him; what else should it be? But what I was sayin' is that it's here he has to come for it, same as Quality after their shootin', and when wunst we've took off wid ourselves, he's no more chanst agin us than they have at a flock of snipe they're after missin' and scarin'. And, signs on it, he's noways wishful to be seein' folk he's plaguin' quit. If it's a young body, now, that's to be took, a bit of a child, or a fine lad, who'll lave plinty breakin' their hearts after them, that belike suits the ould naygur right well, he's nothin' to say agin it; they'll go—they'll go fast enough. But there's a many misfortnit crathurs that onless the Divil does his endeavours to keep them alive in their misery, I dunno who would."

"True for you, ma'am," said Peter Sheridan again, "you might say so, if you'd whiles feel the life was skivered into your body wid all the sharp ends of aches and pains, or else you'd be fit to sthretch yourself out aisy, and away wid you."

"Dunnot say such a thing, then, father," said his daughter Peg, looking piteously at him, and all at once feeling like a parricide, as she bethought her how she had only last night assented to her stepmother's proposition that: Himself was gittin' uglier tempered wid ivery day wint over his head.

"But he's bound to let go a hould of you one time or another, Peter, plase God," Mrs. Kilfoyle urged consolatorily, "whativer villiany he does on you, the end of it is he has to give it up as a bad job, and lave you to go along in paice."

"Arrah now, will no talk contint you but dyin' and the Divil?" remonstrated Mrs. Doyne. "To be hearin' you one ud' think we were just sittin' here a minit to wait till our coffins come up the road, that the ould wan had had the bespakin' of." She glanced furtively round the broad sky-scape, and then huddled herself closer into the shelter of the hollow bank, tightening her skimpy shawl across her shoulders.

"Sure I was manin' no harm wid it," said the old

woman apologetically, " but we might aisy whisht about him for that matter. There's a good few things the Divil has nothin' to say to, or dyin' either, though I dunno why people need mostly think so bad of *that*. It's maybe the sort of throuble there is shiftin' from one place to another that sets thim agin it."

" Aye," said Mrs. Quigley, "some botheration there's apt to be gittin' in and out of anythin', if it's on'y elbowin' your way out of chapel, whin there's a throng at Mass. And 'twill be right at the door you'll git the most crowdin', and pushin', and squeezin,' fit to reive the ould rags off of your back ; but just the next step beyond it, you've all the world clear before you, and room to be dancin' jigs in, if that was what you were after."

" Crowdin', is it?" said Biddy Ryan ; " oh jabers, there's no crowdin' about it that I can see. Musha, it's part of the contrariness of the whole consarn, that so long as you keep livin' there'll be people all about you galore, day out and day in, wid the childer bawlin' and screechin', and the lads quarrelin' and bangin' about, and iverythin' all thro' other under your feet, till you're fairly moidhered, and thinkin' you'd be glad enough to find e'er a little hole away off be yourself for paice and quiet. But whin you come to quittin' them all, and takin' off to nobody can rightly tell where, and you feelin' that quare and lost, you'd be ready to put up wid any company you could git, if it was on'y a brute baste—och then there's niver a sowl you'll have the chanst of along wid you, sorra a mortial one; lonesome or no lonesome, it's be yourself you're bound to go."

"That's the notion young people like you do have," said Mrs. Kilfoyle, who remembered Biddy's grizzled locks as a downy fluff, "but be the time you've lived as long as I, and seen as many comin' and goin'—and stayin' away—you'll find it's behind you that you're lavin' the most of the lonesomeness."

"Seems to me 'twould ha' saved a power of work if God Almighty would ha' been contint to make the one job of it, and stick us all down wheriver it was we were meant to stop, widout any shiftin' us back and forrards," said Andy Sheridan, who had come up with a large turf-creel on his shoulders, and crouching under it on the top of the bank had somewhat the aspect of a straitly-lodged hermit-crab. "It's the same as if you were to be plantin' your pitaties in half a dozen differint places before you'd made your mind up to the right one; and that's a quare way of doin' business."

"P'rhaps you've no call to be in a hurry, me tight lad, to find yourself settled in the place you're bound for," quoth Mrs. M'Gurk, grimly, for Andy was not in her good graces.

"Maybe not," he said, undoubling himself to aim a conjectural cuff at his half-sister Rose, whom he heard trying to tilt over his creel from behind, "but, whether or no, where's the sinse of it?"

"Well, sure, for one thing, if people were to ha' been always in the good place, they mightn't iver know the differ," said Judy Ryan, coming in first, while her neighbours were still casting about for hypotheses.

"And supposin'?" said Andy, swinging his legs unimpressed, "where'd be the harm of not knowin' the differ, when there was nary a differ to know?"

Judy was not prepared to elucidate this point, and looked her perplexity.

"Who said there *was* any sinse in it?" demanded Peter Sheridan, glumly. "As like as not there's none." He was staring straight before him, seemingly in at the black doorway, not many paces distant, out of which he had painfully crawled.

"Ah now, I declare I dare say that's it, glory be to goodness," said Judy, brightening up, as if piously relieved at this solution of the difficulty, "very belike there's no sinse in it *at all;* it's just the will of God."

"And we needn't be consarnin' ourselves about that, anyhow," said Mrs. Quigley.

"Eh, lads dear, we'll all git sorted right enough one way or the other," Mrs. Kilfoyle said, summing up rather hurriedly, for it struck her that the discussion was developing a note of acrimony; "we're better off at all ivints than if we were to be beginnin' wid the good, and endin' wid the bad— And here's Brian after catchin' th'ould hin."

"Bad manners to her then for givin' him such a dance," said Mrs. M'Gurk.

Brian had his captive in a dishevelled wicker basket, from beneath the wobbling lid of which she frequently thrust her witless black head to squawk, at an imminent risk of guillotining, since he suppressed her demonstrations as promptly as if they had been applause in a court of justice.

"Begorrah, ma'am," he said, "if there was anybody down beyant offerin' a stiff price for a sort of ould screech-owl wid springs in the legs of her like a grasshopper's, when she's tired flyin' up over your head like an aigle, you've a right to make your fortin this day. It's lucky I thought to give Norah the hankycher wid the bit of money in it afore she went on, for 'fraid it might git joggled out of me somehow shankin' down. But it's steppin' we ought to be. Good-bye to you kindly, mother; and keep us a sup of hot water boilin'."

The widow twitched away her pig from his grazing, which caused him to exchange his appreciative *hrumphs* for protestant squeals, and they were all three soon out of sight behind the ridge of the knockawn.

"They'll be no great while overtakin' the others at that gait of goin'," said Biddy Ryan. "Och, but 'tis a long draggin' stretch of road, weary on it, and lenthens itself out ivery time you go it. But there's none of us will have tramped it as often as yourself, Mrs. Kilfoyle, ma'am."

"Belike no, me dear," said Mrs. Kilfoyle, "considerin' all the years' start I've had of the whole of yous. Sure I was no age at all, you may say, when first we travelled it. This end of it wasn't rightly finished—faith, Lisconnel was but a poor-lookin' place in those days. And for a while after we did be livin' here, we always called it the road home, because 'twas along it we came out of th'ould place in the county Clare. Then, if we wanted to keep the childer pacified, that was mostly small rampagin' spalpeens, we'd on'y to let on we were settin' out back agin, and they'd trot along till they were tired. But the day me father was buried down beyant, nothin' we could do or say 'ud persuade the crathurs that he hadn't just gone home to fetch our couple of cows. 'Deed, poor man, he fretted terrible after the little black Kerry he left behind—Roseen Dhu he called her. And they did be lookin' out a great while, expectin' him to come dhrivin' her along. D'you see the white stone,

Biddy, up there agin the edge of the headland? That's where little Thady, me youngest brother, 'ud sit watchin' many a day; and had me poor mother disthracted, more-be-token, wid runnin' tumblin' in to her like a bit of a puppy, yellin' that his father was comin' up the road. It's a quare imp of a child Thady was, that wint to the mackerel fishin', and was dhrownded in Galway Bay."

"I just can mind hearin' talk of Thady Joyce," said Peter Sheridan, "but troth, you'll git ahead backwards of the whole of us, ma'am, when it's a matter of recollections."

"Yit for as long as I'm in Lisconnel," Mrs. Kilfoyle said meditatively, "I scarce think I've iver got the idee of it all clare in me head the same way I have the ould place at home. It doesn't seem that nathural to me somehow; lasteways these times when I don't be trapesin' about much, the lie of the lan' gits moidhered up in me mind, as if 'twas wid a mist risin'. But Clonmena, now, sure to this day if I'm lyin' awake in the night, I can be goin' over the whole of it, lighted up in me thoughts, same as I used to, and I a slip of a lass sleepin' in the bit of a room away under the thatch, lookin' out above the front door, wid the river runnin' by. Sure I knew ivery inch of ground it flowed over, and whiles afore I'd fall asleep, I'd divart meself threadin' the fields and all along it, as if you were slippin' your beads thro' your fingers. First it's in our couple of fields, that's the one of them narrer and long-shaped, and the other of them scooped out hollow and round like a sort of nest, and the both of them as smooth and as green as the moss shinin' in the cracks of this ould stone. And then across the end of young Conroy's meadow, below the high bank and the hawthorns atop, and after that off wid it under the dark bridge on the Borrisk road, and spreadin' out on the grey gravel beds, and among the clumps of cress—'tis but a poor hungry bit of land, all tussocks and ragweed—till it runs round the hill-fut among the firs, and gits slitherin' away down and down past the smoothened stones and the brown roots, and the fern-leaves drippin', and the stems tumbled aslant, makin' for the bottom of the deep glen ; and in there it does be shut close wid the trees roofin' it overhead, and the little path wavin' up and down alongside it, all the way to th'ould mill at Kildrum ; so a bit beyond it takes out into the river Coolanagh, no less, that's a powerful width of water. Saints alive, sure I could be follying it along blindfold. Or if it was the win' I heard comin' rustlin' by, the other way, I could tell where it was goin' wid itself— keenin' up the boreen behind the house, and out on the big steep pitatie field, and beyond that agin over the grass slopes, and the sheep browsin', and the breadth of bracken and furze-bushes, till the great cliffs go down at your feet slap into the say like the wall of a church tower. When you look over the edge, you might think there was the white wing of a gull just flutterin' at the bottom, but, musha, all the while it's the foam of a big wave rowled in fit to lift you off your two feet, supposin' you were anywheres it could git a grab at you. You'll hear the sound of them comin' up ivery once and awhile, like as if 'twas the river stoppin' to take breath. But it's the flow of the river I do be missin' most out of it, those times when I'm remimberin' it to meself. I've a notion I'd git a great sleep entirely if iver I come widin sound of it agin. For 'twas the last thing I'd mind afore I dropped off, and as like as not the first thing I'd hear in the mornin' would be our crathurs of ducks flustherin' into it one after the other off of the flat steppin'-stone. And I'd up wid me and out to see to gittin' in the eggs. Goodness guide me, 'twas on'y the other day wakin' up I thought I heard me poor mother callin' 'Chooky, chooky' to her hins, as nathural as could be, and it just Mrs. Pat huntin' home her little goat—I dunno what ould romancin' I have," said Mrs. Kilfoyle, interrupting herself, " but this while back I've nothin' on'y them far-gone days runnin' in me mind. Seems like as if there must be somethin' rael quare ahead of me, that hinders me thinkin' forrards."

"God save you, woman dear, what quareness should there be in it at all?" said Judy Ryan, looking vaguely disquieted ; "why sure, you were always great at remimberin' ; often enough you've tould us the same things afore now ; and it's but nathural. Just as if a body climbin' a hill 'ud be facin' about to look the way he'd come up, for the sake of a rest."

"And there's scarce a one, ould or young," said Biddy Ryan, "but has the feelin' they'd be ready for a good sleep at the day's end, river or no river. Sorra the quareness there's in that. The strongest great big bosthoon of a man that iver stepped," she averred, looking argumentatively at the little old woman, "will be thinkin' of gittin' to sleep when he's tired. There's nothin' like it. Not but what to be sittin' aisy in the sun when you git the chanst this a-way, is mighty agreeable ; isn't it now, ma'am? Look at the light dancin' away yonder on the pool; you might say the water was thinkin' to churn itself into gould and silver."

"Aye, aye, Biddy," said Mrs. Kilfoyle, not looking as far as the bright pool, " 'tis all like a kind of picter to me. But the warmth of the sun does me heart good, and the simmerin'-summerin' there is thro' it, same as if we had the ould kettle sittin' on the hob."

The noontide was indeed going by to an accompaniment of elfin clicking and creaking and whirring, kept up unintermittently on the glowing sward with its tenant grasshoppers and beetles and blue- and red-winged flies, and overborne by a droning boom as often as a dusty bee backed out of one freckled foxglove's purple-shaded cell, and went murmuring to toil and swing in another. Butterflies cruised idly nowhere in particular on white sails, or freaked with orange and scarlet, and mailed dragonflies poised and darted in vivid jewelled gleams. There was scarcely breeze enough stirring to whisk the fuzzy white wigs off the seeded dandelions, and up on the ridge of hill the hot air quivered against the rocks like a curtain about to rise. Lisconnel with its bog lay basking very wide and still, making the most of such a midsummer sun as seldom looks down upon us.

Nothing happened to disturb its quiet perceptibly all the long morning. The neighbours had their dinner when the shadows were shortest, which was the most clearly defined hour of the day for them now that the widow M'Gurk's old clock had given up even pretending to keep time. And then the turf-cutters began again to pass leisurely to and fro, halting with their creels at the bank where the same group had reassembled. So when, well on in the afternoon, Brian Kilfoyle tramped over the hill into Lisconnel, he found everything there very much as he had left it. A grievous change had, however, come over his own frame of mind. He was in a sort of white heat both physically and mentally, what with his long walk in the eye of the sun, and his wrath and consternation; his look showed plainly that some untoward event had brought about his return surprisingly early; for no one had been expected to reappear in such very broad daylight.

"She's lost it on us," he said, confronting his neighbours' interrogative faces with an ironical calm, "the price of the pig; ivery penny of it—that's all."

"Och man alive, don't say so," said his mother.

"Saints and patience, how iver would she happen to go do such a thing?" said Judy Ryan.

"You lie," said Mrs. Quigley, intending to politely convey sympathy mingled with amazement.

"It's truth I tellin' yous," Brian said bitterly. "Sure when we were about comin' on be the Lough shore—and the wark of the warld we had, gittin' that far wid th'ould divilskins of a hin, that kep' her eye cocked to be flyin' out on us ivery step we wint—three several times she got away wid herself, and had Mrs. M'Gurk 'most kilt skirmishin' after her, meself bein' took up conthroulin' the pig—sure there the first thing I beheld was Norah and Nelly stoopin' down lookin' for we couldn't think what along the middle of the road. So sez I to her, when we come up : 'Is it musheroons yous are gatherin' there, woman?' sez I, 'or maybe you'd politefully tell us whether you're weedin' a pitatie-bed or walkin' to the Town.' And wid that she up and began givin' me all sorts for not tyin' the corner of me ould hankycher right, so as the money wouldn't ha' been slippin' out an' goin' to loss along the road. For she'd carried it in her hand the whole way along, niver let go of it for an instiant, and when she thought to be lookin' to see was it all right, and she comin' into the Town, me sowl to the saints if the knot hadn't slipped, and niver a bawbee was tnere left in the blamed ould rag. As regardin' the tyin' now, I'd ha' been ready to take me oath anywhere, and so I tould her, I done it safe enough—But there, have it as you will, we've made a good job of it between the two of us : ivery farthin' gone."

Here everybody pointed out, with slight verbal variations, that if 'twas along the road she'd lost it, he might have a great good chanst of gittin' it yit; any person might be findin' it passin' by.

"Sure I'm just after goin' over ivery step of it," he responded, hopelessly, "and ne'er a trace any more than if they'd been meltin' hailstones. There was the ten-shillin' bit, that's no size at all, it would rowl away into nowhere; I'd niver look to be seein' sight or light of it agin; but I was thinkin' I might be good luck ha' lit on some of the silver and coppers—divil a one. Howsome'er if I'd picked up so much as a couple of the shillins, mother jewel, I'd ha' got you your trifle of tay and sugar, begorrah would I, whativer else might be takin' or lavin', for I think rael bad of you bein' disappointed of it."

"Lord love you, Brian avic, niver go for to be throublin' your mind about any such a thing," piped Mrs. Kilfoyle. She had been, in truth, looking forward incredibly to the fragrant cups of hot tea with which it was an open secret that her son purposed to provide her upon acquiring capital. "I dunno that I've e'er a fancy these times to be drinkin' tay at all. Ah dear, it's a terrible heavy loss on you, so it is, the both of yous, but plase God you might git it agin. And anyways, man dear, there's the goat you'd twinty different minds about sellin', she and a pair of the young hins 'ud mostly fetch you the price of a wee pig, so as you wouldn't be at the loss of a one for fattenin', wid all the waste pitaties comin' in. Sure you're dead beat, child alive, wid trampin' it in the sun's blazes; sit down aisy and be restin' yourself, or maybe you git a bit to ait first in the house."

"But it's steppin' back I must be directly," said

Brian, "and I have a couple of could pitaties in me pocket here if I was wantin' anythin'. If I don't fetch home Norah, she and Nelly 'll be for searchin' the road till this time to-morra."

"Ah, the crathur," said Mrs. Kilfoyle, "she's frettin' herself, you may depind. If you do a bad turn be iver such an accident, you've the feelin 'twas your own fau't all the while, and it's cruel discouragin', forby bein' apt to start you argufyin' and contindin'."

Brian presently set out again through the rich afternoon light with his fallen fortunes. He felt but slightly consoled by his mother's suggestions, and dawdled on slowly, having no sense of a definite object to make him step out. After a while he sat down and ate his cold potatoes, in which, likewise, he found but little solace. Then as, drawing near Classon's Boreen, he was about to turn off the road and take a short cut across a "soft" bit of bog, just passable in dry weather, he became aware of somebody signalling to him on ahead. If the hour had been later, this might have seemed an alarming incident, but in the clear rays where we "scarcely believe much more than we can see," he at once discerned that it was merely Big Anne, clumping along heavily-footed with her marketbasket.

"I wonder to goodness gracious why th'ould

woman can't set the flat of her feet to the ground like a Christian," he said to himself while he went towards her, surveying her ungraceful progress with a censorious eye, his mood being attuned to miscellaneously adverse criticism, "instead of stomp-stompin' that fashion, as if 'twas her notion to drive home a two-inch nail wid aich step she took."

"Have you got it yit, Brian, man?" she inquired as they met.

Brian shook his head. "Nor niver will," he said supplementarily.

"Ah well, you won't be so," Big Anne said with confidence; "it's bound to be somewheres. 'Tisn't as if 'twas a poun'-note that might blow away on you. And here's your bit of tay and sugar," she continued, groping among the contents of her basket. "I thought if that was what you were goin' after, I'd save you a tramp."

"Tay?" repeated Brian, distractedly; "tay? Sure woman, what talkin' have you of tay, and I wid niver the price of a hap'orth left me in creation?"

"'Twould be just borryin' a loan like, till you can put your hand on your money agin, and the mischief take the inconvenience 'twill be to me whativer. Troth, I don't rightly know what I wanted wid gittin' it at all, at all, for Mad Bell she won't touch e'er a drop of it, and it's poor wark, tay-drinkin', when you have it all to yourself. On'y me ould pig wint better than common, and I got a hould of the little fellow Pat Ryan's bringin' along for me surprisin' chape. So it seemed nathural like to git a pound of tay. But then when Mrs. Brian tould me how she was after meetin' the misfortin to mislay all the bit o' money, thinks I to meself it might maybe come in handy for you, supposin' you weren't wishful to disappoint you poor mother of it this evenin', and she belike wid her mind set on havin' a sup. Sure Mrs. Brian was tellin' me she noticed her this mornin' early, dustin' herself a couple of the cups and saucers when she thought no one was mindin', to have them ready. Fit to cry your wife was, too, poor woman, wid the notion she'd be vexed gittin' none; though persuade her I—So I put me best fut forward for 'fraid I'd miss you comin' back. Faith, there's a power of heat yit in that sun!"

" 'Twould be just robbin' you downright, neither more nor less, if we'd take it off of you," said Brian, wistfully eyeing the dark-purple parcels which Big Anne had by this time fished out of her basket. "Thank you kindly all the same, but I couldn't put it on me conscience to——"

A yell suddenly "let" fast by interrupted them, and hurtling towards them over a wet tract of glistening pools came, with kangaroo-like bounds which terminated indifferently in land or water, a Rafferty gossoon.

"Count it," he panted, thrusting something into Brian's hand; "we make it siventeen and fourpince, and ould Mrs. Kilfoyle sez that's right. Whoo, butterfingers—you've dropped two pinnies. Faix, I needn't ha' run the feet off of me legs, if you on'y wanted it to sling about the road."

"Ana where in the name of iverythin' else did you git it at all?" said Brian, staring bewilderedly at his recovered wealth.

"Lyin' in our window at home it was; Nannie's after findin' it just now, comin' in off the bog. They was sayin' you'd likely laid it down out of your hand somehow, afore you started settin' out this mornin'."

"Be the piper, sure enough I was up there splicin' the handle of your mother's ould basket, and it's then I must ha' overlooked it. Och murdher, and me standin' it out to poor Norah that I'd tied it up most particular in the hanky-cher-corner, so as it hadn't a chanst to be slippin' out be any manner of means, I said; and that part of it was true enough. Bedad, she'll be for killin' me alive when she hears tell; but whether or no, I'm a proud man to have it back. I must be trottin on to let her know it's got, for cryin' her eyes out disprit the crathur was the last sight I saw of her. So you perceive I've no call to be throublin' you now about the tay, ma'am; but I'm highly obligated to you all's one."

" And what hour of the day or night might you be expectin' to git home then?" said Big Anne, still holding her rejected packets with a mortified air. " For it's not far from sunsettin' this instiant minit; and be the time you've got down to the Town, and bought your tay and all, and legged it back agin wid Norah and little Nelly, that can't overhurry themselves, 'twill be fine and late. Bedad it's not much tay your mother'll get the drinkin' of this night, if she's to wait for that; she's apt to be in her siventh sleep afore you come."

Brian stood perplexed by conflicting wishes. He wanted to hasten on and relieve his wife's mind, and he wanted his mother to get her tea, and he wanted to have the pleasure of personally presenting it to her. However, the result of his deliberations was that he said: "Well then, if it wouldn't be to inconvanience you, ma'am, I'll axe you to lave it up at our house; she'll know all about it. And that would be what I'm owin' you ma'am"—he counted out the shillings and pennies upon the lid of her basket, and she swept them into it half reluctantly—" but I'm sure I'm much beholden to you; for if it wasn't on'y for you, me mother'd ha' been disappointed of her bit of enjoyment this night any way."

He set off jog-trotting, and Big Anne said to the lad: "Bill, you spalpeen, you'll skyte home a dale quicker than I'll be stumpin' it. Take the bit of tay and sugar along wid you, and lave it at Mrs. Kilfoyle's. Just slip it unbeknownst on to the table, if nobody's in the house, and then when she comes in she'll be findin' it." And as she toiled stiffly along the far-stretching road, a flourish of legs and arms dwindling in front showed her that Bill was speeding on his errand.

Up at Lisconnel, meanwhile, that golden afternoon quietude seemed to close over the perturbing incidents of the loss and recovery of the Kilfoyles' shillings as serenely as the still waters of a sun-shimmering lake close again over a fish's leap. The last ripple of excitement had so died away that the elders were at leisure to notice some slight symptoms of trouble which arose among an adjacent cluster of small children, soon after Bill Rafferty had started in pursuit of Brian. They had been playing peaceably together for a long time in a grassy recess, young Kilfoyles and Quigleys and Ryans, but now some sounds of whimpering distress betokened a marring of harmony.

"Arrah now, what's ailin' yous childer?" inquired Judy Ryan, leaning forward to overlook them from the vantage of a rather higher perch. Whereupon Jim Kilfoyle's whimpering developed into a pronounced howl, while several of his companions replied shrilly : "Jim's after killin' a green beetle—he trod on it runnin' about and kilt it dead."

"And what made him go for to do that?" said Judy, reprovingly ; "sure they're dacint gay-lookin' little things. If it had been any of them black bastes of dowlduffs, now, there'd ha' been some raison in it ; I'd put me fut on one of them meself fast enough, on'y 'twould make me flesh creep to go near it. I thought I was spyin' a sight of one stickin' his hijis head out between them two stones a while ago—Ooch!" Judy gathered her skirts about her shudderingly at the recollection.

"I believe they're but innicint poor crathurs all the while, if they have an ugly appearance on them," said Mrs. Quigley.

"If they were twyste as innicint," Judy persisted, "I wouldn't touch one wid a forty-fut pole. And, morebetoken, I dunno where else they'd ha' got such a way of cockin' up their tails at you, onless they were a sort of divil."

"I *didn't* go for to do it!" Jim said, emerging temporarily from his remorse to vindicate his character. "It ran in right under me feet a purpose, when I was watchin' for it twinklin' in the grass, and I didn't know where it would be comin' to."

"He was the greenest beetle I iver saw," said Rose Ryan, peering at the glitter of emerald, shot with bronze and gold, which Katty Sheridan held ruefully on her palm; "rael purty and shiny he was. That colour'd look lovely in a string of beads."

"And see now what come to him wid it, Rose," said her mother, hortatively. Rising feminine vanity need never suppose that repressive morals will not be drawn for its behoof because it lives remotely in the far west, and goes on bare feet in rags. "Very belike he was that sot up wid thinkin' he was so green and shiny, he didn't mind where he was goin', and there's how he got kilt. If he hadn't been runnin' about as if the whole place was belongin' to him, it might niver ha' happint him at all."

"Maybe if Danny O'Beirne was at home," speculated Joe Quigley, "he could ha' set it goin' agin, same way as he mended up the inside of widdy M'Gurk's ould clock. It wouldn't stir, and nothin' lookin' to be ailin' it, till he gave an odd poke or so to the wheels, and then it wint on grand. And there's no great signs of anythin' broke in the beetle."

"Och, but there's no life left in him whativer,"

pronounced Joe's brother, who had been warily experimenting with a daisy-stalk, " or else he'd be wrigglin' his legs like mad ivery time you'd tickle them."

" His legs do be very black-lookin', mind you,' said Katty, who seemed to consider that this physical trait materially diminished the pathos of the situation. She dropped the creature down on the grass, and the regrets roused by its tragical fate subsided rapidly into oblivion.

Only Jim, the perpetrator of the deed, sat still brooding over it beside the body of the slain, a prey to the limitless remorse of five years old. As the other children moved away from the place, he remained squatting in his dejected attitude so long that his grandmother was struck by it, and said: "What ails Jim, I wonder, not to run about wid the others? He's apt to be gittin' sleepy."

" He's liker to be frettin' yit about disthroyin' of the beetle," said Biddy Ryan. " Jim's unnathural took up wid bastes of the kind. His mother was tellin' me the other day he come into her somewhiles wid his hands full of ladybirds and moths and such, and niver one of them hurted. So he's apt to think bad of killin' anythin'."

"Jim," said old Mrs. Kilfoyle, "I'm goin' in to mind the fire, and when I come out, will I bring you the ould salt-bottle to play wid a bit?"

Jim's state of depression permitted him to nod only a joyless and disconsolate assent. Yet the loan of this article was generally a favour much in request. A relic of the mythical good old days, and the handiwork of Mrs. Kilfoyle's mother, it was a smallish glass bottle, to whose inner sides were mysteriously applied shreds of bright-coloured fabrics, mostly bits of the apple-green chintz which had made her own wedding-gown. The bottle had then been tightly stuffed with salt, which threw out the brilliant hues on a pleasingly white and opaque background; and though now somewhat stained and discoloured by the damps of so many years, it still remained a precious heirloom in the Kilfoyle family, whose resources no longer commanded the productions of decorative art.

"Well, I'll bring it along wid me, honey," said Mrs. Kilfoyle, getting up and standing beside the child, "and if I was you, I'd just cover the poor beetle up comfortable under a scrapeen of moss or somethin' and let it be."

"I'd liefer he'd lave off bein' kilt, and git skytin' about the same way he was before," said Jim, reluctantly accommodating himself to circumstances, and beginning to grub up a tiny velvet sod; "he does be that shinin' in the sun."

"Maybe it might yit," said Mrs. Kilfoyle, "if 'twas left in paice, and not interfered wid. It might ha' come to itself, and you might be watchin' it runnin' about agin, be next summertime. Sure, maybe 'tis no lie I'm tellin' him all the while," the little old woman soliloquised, as she went towards her shadowy doorway with its haze of clear blue smoke, "for it's nary a know I know what's gone wid the spark of plisure did be in the crathur."

That night, not long before the rising of the moon, a great wing of feathery white, which had spread all athwart the sky at sunset, swept away to the east, and the stars, till then visible only glimmer by glimmer, blinking far up behind the drifting plumes, were seen to have mustered in one of their vastest assemblies. The numberless brilliance of their array attracted the notice of two wayfarers who were walking along the bog-road towards Lisconnel, so closely muffled by the rustling darkness round about that to the external world they seemed merely voices and footsteps.

"They've a great ould crop of stars up there this night," said one voice, "and twinklin' fit to thrimble themselves out of their houles."

"Aye," said the other, "I wish I'd as many shillins in me pocket."

"Talkin' of shillins, I wonder did Brian Kilfoyle iver git the hantle of money he was after losin' on the road."

"Och, yis he did, poor man, and a good job too. He's got throubles enough on him this minit widout any more misfortins."

" Why, is there anything gone agin the Kilfoyles lately ? "

" Sure, didn't you hear tell ? The ould mother's just died on him."

" No, bedad. Is it ould Mrs. Kilfoyle ? Och, wirrasthrew, the poor ould woman. And what took her at all ? "

" Faix, I can't tell you. She'd just stepped indoors this evenin' to put her pot on the fire, and some of them comin' in a while afterwards, it's dead they found her there. Sure she was a wonderful great age entirely this long while back The life was ready to flutther away out of her like the bit of down sittin' on a thistle in a waft of win'."

"Eh, but Brian, poor man, he'll be woful put about. He was always thinkin' a hape of th'ould mother. Sure, when I met him down below on'y this mornin', he was in the terriblest takin' at all, because he couldn't be bringin' her some little thrate he'd promised her, be raison of losin' his bit of money. If he'd known but all, he needn't ha' been frettin' himself about that."

" But she got it ; be good luck she got it afore she wint. And belike 'twill be a sort of satisfaction to Brian, and a consowlmint to his mind, that he done her the last thing he had the chanst to. For the time they found her, there she was sittin' wid her ould taypot on her lap, that she'd raiched off the shelf, and she'd the poun' parcel of tay opened, as if she was intindin' to wet herself a drop."

" Och now, the crathur, to think of that—Whisht —me sowl—whisht man; what was that we heard?"

" What was it ? Nothin' but a plover pipin' away over be the lough. 'Tis a powerful dark night, considerin' the sight of stars that are out on it; howsome'er the moon 'll be risin' afore you're home. Bedad, there she is about gittin' up wid herself yonder, where the light sthrake's showin', like as if you'd been scrapin' a match agin a wall."

" So she is. Prisintly she'll be swimmin' up meltin' herself in the light like a bit of ice in clear water, same as she was last night, and then I'll pick me way back finely. Poor Mrs. Kilfoyle Heaven shine on her sowl in glory. The dacint poor old body she was, and always wid a good word for ivery one. They'll be rael annoyed to hear tell of it at our place. And you'll be missin' her many a day up at Lisconnel ; it's a great opinion yous all had of her entirely."

" Faith and we had then, little and big. But

anyway she's got the best of it over us. We'll do well enough, if so be we've the luck to slip off as aisy when we come to quittin'."

" Aye, will we, plase God."

CHAPTER X.

COMING AND GOING.

THE summer following Mrs. Kilfoyle's death was, what with one thing and another, a drearyish season at Lisconnel. That little old woman had left a great gap, and there came many long spells of gloomy, bad weather, which seemed to beat people's troubles down upon them as the damp drove the turf-reek back through their smoke-holes into the dark rooms, where they could not see how dense the blue haze was growing. Stacey Doyne's marriage also had removed something young and pleasant, and at times, when the thatch dripped without and within, neighbours were apt to talk about her in tones of commiseration, and say, " Sure her poor mother's lost entirely." So that towards autumn the distraction of some new residents' arrival happened rather opportunely. It was made possible by the fact that Big Anne had given up her holding and entered into partnership with the widow M'Gurk, thus leaving her late abode empty for another tenant, who appeared much sooner than any one might have anticipated from the aspect of the cabin.

Except as a fresh topic of conversation, however, the strangers gave small promise of proving an acquisition to the community. Lisconnel did not like their appearance by any means, and further acquaintance failed to modify unfavourable first impressions. These were mainly received in the course of the day after their arrival, which took place on a night too black for anything beyond a shadowy counting of heads, and a perception that the bulk of the new-comers' household stuff had jogged up on one donkey, and must therefore be small. A portion of Big Anne's furniture had remained behind her in the cabin, owing to certain arrears of rent; her heart was scalded, she said, wid the prices she'd only get for her early chuckens, and they the weight of the world, if you'd feel them in your hand; and poor Mad Bell, that 'ud mostly bring home a few odd shillins wid her, was away since afore Christmas, and might never show her face there agin, the crathur—a bit of narration which would look funny enough in anybody's rental. Mrs. Quigley, who went to the door with the offer of a fire-light, found it shut, and a voice inside said, "as onmannerly as you plase, 'No, we've matches,'" whereupon another voice, further in the interior, quavered, "Thank'ee kindly." So she departed little wiser than she had come. But daylight showed that the party consisted of an old man, and his son, and his son's wife, and her sister, and three small children; besides some cochin-china fowl, and a black cat with vividly green eyes. This much was apparent on the surface. Also that the old man was frail, bent, shrivelled, and civil spoken, that the son was "a big soft gomeral of a fellow," that both the women were sandily flaxen-haired, with broad flat cheeks and light eyes, that two of the children resembled them in an infantine way, and that the third, a girl a trifle older, was a dark-haired, disconsolate-looking little thing, "wid her face," Mrs. Brian said, "not the width of a ha'penny herrin', and the eyes of her sunk in her head." As for the fowl, there could be no doubt that their "onnathural long flufferty legs were fit to make a body's flesh creep," and the cat looked "as like an ould divil as anythin' you ever witnessed, sittin' blinkin' atop of the turf-stack."

Other less self-evident facts came out by degrees, slower than might have been expected, as the strangers were generally close and chary of speech. They came from the north, where their affairs had not prospered; in fact, they had been "sold up and put out of it," as the young man divulged one day to Brian Kilfoyle. They were a somewhat intricately connected family, by the name, predominantly, of Patman. The sister-in-law was Tishy M'Crum, which seemed simple enough; but the two light-haired boys were Greens, Mrs. Patman having been a widow, while the little girl was the child of a wife whom Tom Patman had already buried, for though he looked full young to have embarked upon matrimony at all, this was his second venture. "And it's a quare comether she must ha' been after puttin' on him," quoth Mrs. Quigley, "afore he took up wid herself, that's as ugly as if she was bespoke, and half a dozen year oulder than the young bosthoon if she's a minnit." It is true that at the time when Mrs. Quigley expressed this unflattering opinion she and her neighbours had been exasperated by an impolite speech of Mrs. Patman, who had said loudly in their hearing: "Well for sartin, if I'd had a notion of the blamed little dog-hole he was bringin' us into, sorra the sole of a fut 'ud I ha' set inside it;" and had then proceeded to congratulate herself upon having left all her dacint bits of furniture up above at her mother's, so that she needn't be bothered wid cartin' them away out of a place that didn't look to have had ever e'er a thing in it worth the trouble of movin', not if it stood there until it dropped to pieces wid dirt. Mrs. Quigley rejoined that it would be a great pity if any people sted in a place that wasn't good enough for them, supposin' all the while they knew of e'er a better one; maybe they might, or maybe they mightn't. It was won'erful to hear the talk some folks had, wid every ould stick they owned an aisy loodin' for Reilly's little ass. But Judy Ryan with a flight of sarcastic fancy hoped that Mrs. Patman and her family were about goin' on a visit to the Lady Lifftinant, because it was much if they'd find any place else where there'd be grandeur accordin' to their high-up notions.

Skirmishes such as this, however, were a symptom rather than a cause of the Patmans' unpopularity. That sprang from several roots. For one thing, both the women had harsh, scolding voices, and it was even chances that if you passed within earshot of their cabin you would hear them giving tongue. Their objurgations were as a rule addressed to the young man or the old, the latter of whom presently grew into an object of local compassion, as "a harmless dacint poor crathur," while his son came in for the frank-eyed looking down upon which is the portion of an able-bodied man shrew-ridden through sheer supineness and "polthroonery." But what Lisconnel often said that it "thought badder of" was the stepmotherly treatment which seemed to be the lot of the little girl Katty. Of course the situation was one which under the circumstances would have made people believe in such a state of things upon the slenderest evidence. Still, even to unprejudiced eyes it was clear that Katty's rags were raggeder than those of her small stepbrothers, and that she crept about with the mien of a creature which has conceived reasonable doubts respecting the reception it is likely to meet in society. When the autumn weather began to grow wintry, little Katty Patman, "perishin' about out there in the freezin' win'," became a spectacle which was viewed with indignant sympathy from dark doorways whence she received many an invitation to step in and be warmin' herself. Her hostesses opined that she was fairly starved just for a taste of the fire, and didn't believe she was ever let next or nigh it in her own place. Often, too, the consideration that she had no more flesh on her bones than a March chicken led to the bestowal of a steaming potato, or a piece of griddle-bread; but the result of this was sometimes unsatisfactory to the giver, Katty being apt to dart away with her refreshments, which she might presently be seen sharing among Bobby and Hughey, for whom she entertained a strong and apparently unreciprocated regard.

"I wouldn't go for to be sayin' anythin' to set

her agin them," Mrs. Brian remarked on some such
occasion, " but, goodness forgive me, I've no likin'
for them two little brats; I misthrust them."

"Ah sure they've no sinse," said Biddy Ryan;
"where'd they git it, and the biggest of them, I'd
suppose, under four years ould?"

"Sinse?" said Mrs. Quigley. "Bedad, thin, if
sinse was all that ailed them, the pair of them is as
cute as a couple of foxes. I mind a day or so after
they'd been in it, I met the laste one on the road,
and I comin' home wid bechance a sugar-stick in
me baskit. So just to be makin' friends like, I gave
it a bit for itself, and a bit for the other, that I seen
comin' along. Well now, ma'am, if it had took
and eat up the both bits, I'd ha' thought ne'er a
pin's point of harm; 'twould ha' been nathural
enough to the size of it. But I give you me word,
when it seen it couldn't get the two of them swal-
lied down afore its brother come by, what did it go
do but clap the one of them into a crevice in the
wall, and cover it under a blackberry laif. And
wid that doun it squats and begins sayin': 'Creely-
crawly snail—where's the creely-crawly snail I'm
after huntin' out of its hole?' Lettin' on to be
lookin' for somethin' creepin' in the grass. And a
while after it came slinkin' back, when it thought
nobody was mindin', to poke the bit out of the
wall, where I was gatherin' dandelions under the

bank. So while it was fumblin' about, missin' the right crevice, sez I, poppin' up, thinkin' to shame it: 'Maybe the crawly snail's after aitin' it on you,' sez I. 'Och yis, I seen it,' sez the spalpeen, as brazen as brass. 'Gimme noder bit instid.' There's a schemin' young rapscallion for you."

"They're too like their mother altogether," said Judy Ryan; "the corners of their eyes do be as sharp as if they were cut out wid a pair of scissors. Not that I'd mind if they'd e'er a sthrake of good-nature in them; but I misdoubt they have. The little girl, now, is as diff'rint as day and night."

"If *she* takes after her father, she's a right to want the wit powerful, misfortnit little imp," said Mrs. Brian; "for if he isn't a great stupid gomeral and an ass, just get me one. Why, if he was worth pickin' out of a dry ditch, he'd purvint of his own child bein' put upon."

"Och, they have him *frighted*," said Mrs. Quigley, with scornful emphasis; "they won't let him take an atom of notice of her, they're that jealousy. Sure, if he gets talkin' to her outside the house there, one of them 'ill let a bawl and send him off to be carryin' in turf or wather; I've seen it times and agin."

"If he'd take and sling it about their ears some fine day, he'd be doin' right, and it might larn them to behave themselves," said Judy.

"But the ould man would disgust you," said Mrs. Quigley, " wid the romancin' he has out of him about his son Tom. You'd suppose, to listen to him, that the omadhawn's aquil never stepped. He'll deive you wid it till you're fairly bothered. Troth, he thinks the young one's doin' somethin' out of the way if he just walks down the street, and expecs everybody to stand watchin' him goin' along. It's surprisin' the foolery there does be in people."

" Och murdher, women alive," said Ody Rafferty, whose pipe went out at this moment, "there's no contintin' yous at all. It's too cute they are, and too foolish they are. Musha, very belike they're not so much off the common, if you'd a thrifle more experience of them; there's nothin' to match that for evenin' people. Bedad, now, there's some people *I* know so well that I can scarce tell the one from the other."

Lisconnel, however, generally declined to fall in with Ody's philosophical views, and the Patmans, whether suspected of excessive cuteness or folly, remained persistently unpopular. There was only one exception to this rule. The widow M'Gurk has a certain fibre of perversity in her, which sometimes twists itself round unlikely objects, for no apparent reason save that they are left clear by her neighbours; and this peculiarity renders her prone upon occasion to undertake the part of Devil's Advocate. When, therefore, she had once delivered herself of the opinion that the newcomers were "very dacint folks," she did not feel called upon to abandon it because it stood alone. As grounds for it she commonly alleged that they were "rael hard-workin' and industhrious," which was obviously true enough, since Mrs. Patman and her sister might constantly be seen tilling their little field with an energy far beyond the capacity of its late tenant. Her neighbours' unimpressed rejoinder, "Well, and supposin' they are itself?" did not in the least disconcert the widdy, nor yet their absence of enthusiasm when she stated that it was "a sight to behould Tishy M'Crum diggin' over a bit of ground; she'd lift as much on her spade as any two men." As for little Katty, "she'd never seen anybody doin' anythin' agin the child; it might happen by nature to be one of those little *crowls* of childer, that 'ud always look hungry-like and pinin', the crathurs, if you were able to keep feedin' them wid the best as long as the sun was in the sky." In short, something more than talk was usually needed to put the widow M'Gurk out of conceit with any notion she had taken up. Perhaps the comparative aloofness of her hill-side cabin helped to maintain the Patmains at their original high level in her estimation. At any rate, they had not sunk from it by the time that they had been nearly three months in Lisconnel, and when Mrs. Patman and her sister were on terms of the very glummest civility with all the other women in the place. Even towards the widow M'Gurk they were tolerant rather than expansive; she said, "They done right enough not to be leppin' down people's throaths."

One morning not long after Christmas, the widow, being bound on an errand down below, called in at the Patmans' with a view to possible commissions. Meal was wanted, and while Tishy M'Crum stitched up a rent in the bag Mrs. M'Gurk noticed where little Katty, who had been "took bad wid a could these three days," rustled uncomfortably among wisps of rushes and rags in an obscure corner. Fever made her bold and self-assertive, for she was wishing nothing less than that her daddy would get her an orange. "An or'nge wid yeller peel round it"—Katty laid stress on this point—like the one her mammy got her a long time ago. And daddy'd be a good daddy and get her another now. And she'd keep a bit for Bobby and Hughey and all of them.—A big yeller or'nge. Katty's eyes blazed with excitement as she reiterated these desires.

"She's got an uncommon fancy for a one," said her daddy, looking wistfully from the child to his wife.

"They have them down below," suggested the widow, "pence a piece."

Mrs. Patman's hand was slipping towards her pocket: "If it was just for onst"—she had begun, when Tishy tweaked her sleeve viciously, and interpolated a rapid whisper: "It won't *be;* there'll be no ind to it if you begin humourin' them;" so the sentence was badly dislocated. "She'll do a dale better widout any such thrash," said Mrs. Patman, and walked off to throw sods on the fire.

Just then the widow became aware that old Joe Patman was grimacing at her from a corner fast by in a way which might have startled her had she not been familiar with such modes of beckoning. But when she obeyed his summons, what she saw astounded her outright, for Joe was stooping over a leathern pouch, which he had drawn from a wall-cranny, and which seemed to contain marvellous depths of silver money, with here and there a golden gleam among it, as he warily stirred it up, circling a hurried forefinger. She had only the briefest glimpse ere he shoved back the pouch and thrust a sixpence into her hand, muttering, "Git her the orange—don't be lettin' on, for your life." As she turned away with a reassuring nod, she perceived that Tishy M'Crum was standing unexpectedly near, and looking towards them over the top of the meal-bag. Tishy was biting off a loose end of thread, which gave her a determined and ferocious expression, but whether she could have seen anything or not the widow felt uncertain. She thought not.

About ten days after this, Mrs. M'Gurk was roused at a very early hour by a thumping on her door. When she opened it, she found some difficulty in recognising her visitor, as the dawn had scarcely done more than dim a few stars far away in the east, which is an ineffective form of illumination. "Whethen now, Joe Patman, is it yourself?" she said peeringly. "And what's brought you out at all afore you can see a step or a stim? Is the little girl took worse?" For Katty's illness still continued and had grown rather serious.

"Sure no," said the old man; "Katty's just pretty middlin'. But it's waitin' I've been the len'th of the mornin', till 'twould turn broad daylight, before I'd be disturbin' of you, ma'am, to tell you the quare sort of joke they're after playin' on me down yonder."

"Saints above, man, what talk have you of jokin' at this hour of the day or night?" said Mrs. M'Gurk, feeling the unseasonableness acutely, as a bitter gust came swooping up the slope, and indiscriminatingly ruffled the rime-dusted grass-tufts and her own grizzled locks.

"Och bejabers, it's a great joke they have agin me whatever," said old Patman, who was shivering much, with cold partly, and partly perhaps with amusement. "You see the way of it was, last night, no great while after we'd all gone asleep, I woke up suddint, like as if wid the crake of a door, or somethin', but whatever it might be, 'twas slipped beyond me hearin' afore I'd got me sinses rightly. So I listened a goodish bit, and somehow everythin' seemed unnathural quite, till I heard Katty fidgettin', and I went over to see would she take a dhrink of wather. The Lord presarve us and keep us, ma'am, if all the rest of them hadn't quit—quit out of it they have, and left us clever and clane."

"Ah now, don't be romancin', man," said the widow, remonstrantly. "What in the name of the nation 'ud bewitch any people to go rovin' out of their house in the middle of the black night, wid the frost thick on the ground?"

"Quit they are," said the old man. "Tom's gone, and the wife, and every man jack of them. They've took the couple of chuckens I noticed Tishy killin' of yisterday—begorrah, I believe they've took Tib the cat, for ne'er a sign of it I see about the place, that would mostly be sittin' cocked up on the dresser. Goodness guide us, sorra a sowl there is in the house but the two of us, me and the child, and she's rael bad. It's a quare ould joke."

"It 'ud be the joke of a set of ravin' mad people," said the widow.

"But the best of it is," he went on, "do you mind, ma'am"—he looked round him suspiciously and lowered his voice—"the leather pooch you might ha' seen wid me the other day?"

"Whoo!" said Mrs. M'Gurk, "are they after takin' that on you? Sure, man, I thought you had it unbeknownst."

"Aye, it's took," old Patman said; "but how she grabbed it I dunno, unless, I was thinkin', be any chance you mentioned somethin' about it."

"Divil a bit of me did," averred the widow, with truth, which her hearer accepted; "and how much might you have had in it at all?"

"Troth, I couldn't be tellin' you," he said, "I never thought to count it. 'Tis just for a pleasure to meself I keep it. This long while back I've put ne'er a penny in it, but when we used to be livin' up at Portnafoyle, I'd slip in the odd shillins now and agin, and sometimes I'd think 'twould be handy for buryin' me, and other times I'd think I'd give it to Tom as soon as I'd gathered a trifle more, on'y some way the thought of partin' wid it 'ud seem to go agin me, and since poor Tom made a match wid Martha M'Crum, 'tis worse agin me it goes. 'Tis that good-for-naught weasel of a slieveen Tishy's after conthrivin' it on me," quoth the old man, with a sudden spasm of resentment. " Tom 'ud never play such a thrick—I mane it wasn't he invinted the joke; he doesn't throuble himself much wid jokin'; he's too sinsible, and steady, and perspicuous, and uncommon set on me and the child. There's no better son in Ireland. Och, but the rest of them mane no harm wid it; they're just schemin' to drop in presintly and be risin' a laugh on me."

Steps which were promptly taken to verify old Joe Patman's strange story proved it to be correct in every particular. The only fresh fact which they brought to light was the presence of a fiveshilling piece lying on the dresser, where Joe had overlooked it in the early dusk. All the other inmates, chuckens and cat included, had disappeared, and with them most of the few movables; the old man and the sick child being left as forlorn fixtures. Lisconnel at large was neither slow nor circumlocutory in forming and expressing its opinion as touching the nature of the joke, a firm belief in which old Joe resolutely opposed to his troubles as they thickened around him. For no tidings came from the absentees or were heard of them, while

Katty's fever ran so high that it seemed likely he would be at small further charges on her account—a prospect which, however financially sound for a capitalist of five shillings or under, none the less filled his soul with grief. Then, one night, when Katty was at her worst, a great gale came rushing and roaring across the bog, and when the day broke, it discovered the Patmans' brown thatch-slope interrupted by a gaping crevasse, over which a quick-plashing rain-sheet quivered.

The widow M'Gurk had less spare room than heretofore at her disposal now that she harboured a co-tenant, with a slight accession of tables and chairs. Yet she made out a dry corner for the child and her grandfather, who accepted these quarters in preference to any others, because the widow, whatever may have been her private views, was prevented by a mixture of contrariness and magnanimity from joining in the general denunciation of her former allies, compromising as were the circumstances under which they had elected to take their departure. In her society, therefore, he was not fain to overhear trenchant criticisms upon Tom's behaviour, and could dilate, at least uncontradicted, upon those gifts and graces in the young man which recent events had placed in some need of exposition. Other disquieting voices there were, however, which he could not dodge, and they spoke louder every day. For his five shillings were melting, dwindling—had vanished; and Lisconnel, with the best will in the world, could ill brook a burden of two incapables more laid upon its winter penury. No word on the subject had reached the old man's outer ears, but as Katty struggled slowly and fractiously towards convalescence, it became clearer in his mind that unless something happened, she must, when well enough to be moved, seek change of air away at the big House. Perhaps this prospect was more constantly before him than even the thought of Tom's filial virtues, as he sat drearily on the bank by widow M'Gurk's door. He might often be seen to shake his head despondently, and then he was saying to himself: "Belike he thought bad of me keepin' the bit of money unbeknownst."

By that time he had abandoned the joke theory, and fixed his hopes upon the arrival of a letter to explain the mysterious nocturnal flitting, and say whither they had betaken themselves after passing through Duffclane, the furthest point to which the detective forces of the district had tracked the party. Young Dan O'Beirne, whose work brought him daily up from down below to the forge halfway towards Lisconnel, had safely promised to convey this letter so far whenever it came; and on many a day the neighbours nodded commiseratingly to one another as they saw "the ould crathur settin' off wid himself" in quest of it. The prompt January dusk would have already fallen before he struggled up the knockawn, to be greeted by the widow in the tone of marked congratulation which our friends sometimes adopt when all reason for it is conspicuously absent: "Well, man alive, there wouldn't be e'er a letter in it this day anyway."

"Och, tubbe sure, not at all," he would answer cheerfully. "I wouldn't look to there bein' e'er a one sooner than to-morra. I hadn't the notion of expectin' a letter whatever. 'Twas just for the enjoyment of the bit of a walk I went."

"Why, tubbe sure it was. But be comin' in, man, for you're fit to drop, and be gettin' your ould brogues dried. Och, man, you're dhrounded entirely; 'tis a mighty soft evenin' it's turnin' out."

"And here's Katty lookin' out for you this great while," Big Anne would say; "she's finely this night, glory be to goodness."

Affairs were much in this posture, when the widow was one day perplexed by the occurrence of two small incidents. In the first place, as she was starting on an expedition to the town she saw at a little distance something run across the road which looked uncommonly like the Patmans' black cat Tib. Lisconnel owns no other cats for which she might have mistaken it; still, as she was puzzled to think how the creature should have hidden itself away for more than a fortnight, she concluded that she had been deceived by some fluttering bird or glancing shadow. In the next place, she happened in the town upon one Larry Donnelly, who in the course of conversation remarked: "So you've that young Patman back wid yous agin. What took him to be leggin' off wid himself that way?"

"And what put that in your head at all?" said the widow. "Light nor sight we've seen of him, or a one of them, or likely to. It's off out of the counthry he is, belike, and he after robbin' his ould father, that's niver done talkin' foolish about him, and lavin' his innicent child to go starvin' into the Union—bad luck to him." She found a free expression of her sentiments rather refreshing after the restrictions under which she was placed at home.

"Well, now," said Donnelly, "I'd have bet me pair of best brogues I seen that chap a couple of nights ago streelin' along the road down about our place; but 'twas darkish enough, and I might aisy be mistook."

The widow pondered much over this statement on her homeward way, but had the forbearance to say nothing about it. She was still undecided whether or no she would communicate it to anybody, when, next morning, on her way for a can of water, she saw the black cat, unmistakable this time, run across the road, and, as on the day before, make off over the bog towards the little river. Widow M'Gurk stood staring after it for a few minutes, and came to a resolution. Then she looked about her, and was aware of Andy Sheridan's head leaning against his doorpost. Of Andy her opinion was, as we have seen, rather low, but she could descry no other person available for her purpose, so she called to him: "Andy lad, I'm goin' after me two pullets that's strayed on me; come and be givin' me a hand." Andy lounged over to her good-naturedly, and they turned into the bog, where Ody Rafferty presently joined them. The widow thought her fowl might be among the broken ground, where the stream runs at the back of the knockawn, and the three went in that direction. It was a mild, soft, grey morning, and they met with neither stir nor sound, till they came abruptly upon a grassy hollow, shut in by furzy banks, and fronted by the running water; and then the widow, who alone had been expecting the unexpected, uttered a suppressed screech, and said: "Och boys dear, goodness gracious guide us!"

What they saw was the figure of a man in a long great-coat, "crooched all of a hape" under the bank. Near him were ranged in a row half a dozen oranges, striking up a wonderful golden glow. A small grimy scrap of paper was spread out near them, covered with several piles of shillings and pennies, and a silver thimble. Beside these Tib the black cat sat severely tucked up, apparently dissatisfied and irked by the situation. At the widow's exclamation the man raised his head, and was seen to be Tom Patman, looking haggard and dazed, and as hollow-eyed as little Katty herself. Widow M'Gurk and Ody and Andy stood in a line facing him.

"Whethen now, Tom Patman," said Ody, "and what might *you* be doin' wid yourself?"

"I'm sittin' here," said Tom.

"Och musha, tell us somethin' we don't know then. Sittin' there you are, sure enough, but what the mischief are you after, might I politely ax? or what you mane *by* it, at all at all?"

"I'm sittin' here," said Tom again, "and starvin' I am; and sittin' and starvin' I'll be morebetoken till the end of me ould life. Sure what else 'ud I be doin', and meself to thank for it, wid never a sowl left belongin' me in the mortial world, nor a place to be goin' to?"

"Well, tubbe sure," said Mrs. M'Gurk, "if that talk doesn't bate all that ever I heard! And himself after trapesin' off as permiscuous as an ould hin that won't sit on her eggs, and lavin' his own flesh and blood behind him as if they were the dust on the road. And then he ups and gives chat about niver a sowl bein' left him."

" 'Twas Tishy—bad cess to her," said Tom. " Och, but it's the mischievous ould divilskins is Tishy M'Crum; and it's herself stirred up Martha, that wouldn't be too bad altogether if she'd be let alone, till the two of them had me torminted wid tellin' me th' ould man had pots of money he'd niver spend as long as he had us to be livin' on; and that we'd all do a dale better if some of us slipped away aisy widout risin' a row, and left him for a bit, while we'd be sellin' Martha's things, and seein' about gettin' into a dacint little place, instid of the whole of us to be starvin' alive up at Lisconnel, that's nothin' more than a bog bewitched; and he after lettin' us be sold up, they said, and all the while ownin' mints of money, so that we'd no call to be overly partic'lar about lavin' him to make a shift along wid the child, if 'twas a convenience, on'y he'd be risin' a quare whillabaloo if he knew we were goin' anywhere. Troth, I couldn't tell you the gabbin' they had day and night—and showin' me the place he kep' his bag hidden in— and this way and that way. Och bedad, themselves 'ud persuade the hair on your head it grew wrong side out, if they'd a mind to it."

"They might so," said Ody, "supposin' I was great gomeral enough to be mindin' a word they'd say or the likes of them." In his subsequent reports of the interview, Ody always alleged that he had replied: "Aye, very belike, supposin' it grew on the head of an ass," which was certainly neater. But Ody Rafferty's repartees, like those of other people, are occasionally belated in this way.

"So the ind of it was," Tom went on, "nothin' else 'ud suit them except gettin' all readied up for us to be slinkin' out in the evenin' late. Faith, I'd twenty minds in me heart agin quittin' little Katty, and she that bad. Howane'er, they swore black and white that me father'd be spendin' all manner of money on her when he got us out of it, and we were to be writin' for them to come after us as soon as we were settled, and everythin' agreeable—so I went along. But if I did, ma'am, sure when they'd got the bits of furniture sold, the on'y notion they had was to be settin' off to make fortins in the States, and ne'er a word about Katty and the ould man. Och, they had me disthracted; outrageous they were; and that ould thief of the world Tishy allowin' me sorra a penny, so as I mightn't ha' been bound to stop where I was. But one day they thought they had me asleep in the room-corner, and the two of them was colloguin' away at the table, so all of a suddint Tishy whips out me poor father's bag, that I knew the look of right well, when he used to keep his baccy in it, and down she slaps it, and it jinglin' wid money. 'What's that for you?' sez she, and, 'The laws, bless us,' sez Martha, 'is it after takin' that you are? And what's to become of them crathurs up at Lisconnel?' 'Och blathers,' sez Tishy, 'you needn't be lettin' on you didn't well know all this while I had it. Sure th' ould one might ha' plinty more hidden on us. Anyway, I left them somethin' to git along wid,' sez she—"

"The five shillins," said the widow. "Och, but that one's a caution."

"Rael hard-workin' and industhrious she is," observed Andy.

"'Thim two'll do as well inside as out,' sez Tishy. 'I'll just be countin' the bit of silver,' sez she. But bedad I was fairly past me patience, and up I leps, and I grabbed a hould of the little bag. Och, it's a quare fright I gave them that time, and they not thinkin' I was mindin', rael terrified they were," said Tom, sitting up more erect, and recalling this rare experience with evident complacency. "And 'Lave that, you omadhawn,' sez Tishy, wid the look of a divil on her. 'What foolery are you at now?' 'You thievin' miscreant,' sez I, 'it's shankin' off to the polis I'll be, and layin' a heavy charge agin you for robbin' and stealin', and you after lavin' the child there and the ould man to starve widout a penny to their names,' sez I. 'Faugh!' sez she; 'for that matter, the fever's liker to have took her off wid no throuble to be starvin', and maybe a good job too for everybody.' And 'Be this and be that,' sez I, 'if I thought there was e'er a fear of it,' tis wringin' your ugly neck round I'd be this instiant.' 'Let go of that bag,' sez she, sweepin' up some of the shillins that was spilt. 'The polis,' sez I, 'and a heavy charge, if there's another word out of your hidjis head.' 'I vow and declare,' sez Martha, 'I believe 'twould be the chapest thing we could do wid him, to let him take it and go. Sure he'd be divil a ha'porth more use for an imigrint than the ould cat there I was ape enough to bring along to pacify the childer.' So then Tishy gave some more impidence, but the last end of it was we come to an agreement that I'd take the note and the silver and they'd keep what bits of gould was in it, and they'd go off wid themselves wherever they plased at all, and I'd tramp straight back here to be lookin' after the child and th' ould man. Aye bedad, we settled it up civil enough. And afore I went Martha handed me out th' ould thimble, and bid me be bringin' it to Katty. ''Twas her mother's,' sez she, 'I was keepin' for her; and thick it is wid holes be the same token, but don't say I'd be robbin' it off of her.' And they tould me to take Tib along, or else they'd be lavin' her to run wild ; so I put her in the basket. Begorrah, I believe Hughey had a notion to be comin' wid me and the cat, for he was lettin' woful bawls the last thing I heard of him.

" So away I come wid the best of me haste; och, I knocked the quare walkin' out of meself entirely. And I stopped at the last big place I was passin' to get Katty the oranges. And I was trampin' it all the night after, till just when there was a sthrake of the mornin' over the bog, I come into Lisconnel. But och wirra wirra—the roof's off of the house—och, the look of the black hole wid the rafters stickin' through it, and ne'er a breath of smoke, till me heart was sick watchin' to see might there be an odd one, and the door clap-clappin'. Sure, be that I well knew the child was dead, and me father quit out of it, or maybe buried himself, and I after lavin' them dyin' and starvin'. So for 'fraid somebody'd be comin' out and tellin' me, off I run away into the bog, till I was treadin' here in the could wather. And then I tumbled th' ould cat out of the basket, that was scrawmin' and yowlin' disp'rit, and I slung the basket into the sthrame—there's the handle among them rushes—and down I sat under the bank. I dunno how many nights and days it is at all—but here I'll stop; never a fut I'll stir to be lookin' for bite or sup, or lettin' on I'm in it—and anybody may take the bit of money and welcome; I'd as lief be pickin' up the dirt on the road—for I'll just give me life a chanst to end out of the world's misery and disolation."

"Now may goodness forgive you," said the widow M'Gurk, "it's a poor case to want the wit. Troth, and yourself's the quare ould child-desertin', mane-spirited, aisy-frighted slieveen of a young bosthoon; but what sort of a conthrivance is it you have on you at all at all be way of a head that you couldn't have the sinse to consider the roof blowin' off of a body's house 'ud be raison enough for them to be quittin' out of it, and no sign of dyin' in the matter? D'ye think the win' was apt to be waitin' till there happened to be nobody widin, afore it got scatterin' the thatch? God help us all, you've little to do to be squattin' there talkin' about disolations and miseries, wid the two of them this instiant minnit sittin' be the fire up at my place, and sorra a hand's turn ailin' them, forby Katty's a thrifle conthrary now and agin, through not bein' entirely strong yit."

"And bedad at that hearin'," reports of the occurrence used to proceed from this point, "the lep he gathered himself up with, and the rate he legged it off—musha, he was over the hill while we were pickin' up his things for him. And as for th' ould cat that he tipped over, it rowled a perch of ground before it got a hould of its four feet."

"Sure we were sittin' there as quite as could be consaived"—the conclusion of this precipitate rush was thus recounted—" when all of a suddint we couldn't till what come bouncin' in at the door as if it had been shot out of the ends of the earth, and had us all jumpin' up and screechin', till we seen it was on'y Tom Patman, and he in such a takin' you might suppose he thought somethin' 'ud swally up ould Joe and the child on him before he could get at them."

Lisconnel's opinion was divided as to whether Tom would actually have stayed and starved in his hiding-place had he not been discovered. Mrs. M'Gurk thought it likely enough. "The cat goin' back and for'ards that way," she said, "gave her an idee there was somethin' amiss in it, and that was why she took Andy along. 'Deed and she got a quare turn when first she spied the chap croochin' under the bank—she couldn't tell but he might ha' been a corp." Brian Kilfoyle's view was: "Divil a much! Sure if he'd had e'er a notion to be doin' anythin' agin himself, there was plenty of deep bog holes handy for him to sling himself into, and have done wid it." Whereupon

Mrs. Sheridan crossed herself deprecatingly, and said: "Ah sure, belike the crathur wouldn't have the wickedness in him to go do such a thing." Her husband didn't know but he might. "Them soft sort of fellers 'ud sometimes stick to anythin' they took into their heads, the same as a dab of morthar agin a wall." And Ody Rafferty supposed the fact of the matter was "that if be any odd chanst they got a notion of their own, they mistook it for somebody else's."

On one point, however, the neighbours, Mrs. M'Gurk not excepted, were practically unanimous, the utter flagitiousness, namely, of Tishy M'Crum. There was a tendency to begrudge her the trivial merit of having voluntarily left behind her the five-shilling piece, as this marred that perfect symmetry of iniquity which is so pleasant to the eye when displayed by people of whom we "have no opinion." Only Mrs. Brian said it was a mercy she had that much good-nature in her itself; but even she added that the fewer of them kind of folks she saw comin' about the place the better she'd be plased; and she hoped they'd got shut of them for good and all.

This aspiration seemed the more likely to be fulfilled when within a week or so the Patmans heard from the family of Tom's first wife, who held out prospects of work for himself and a home for his father and Katty—an offer which was gladly accepted. Their departure left, as the single trace of their sojourn in Lisconnel, Tib the cat, which remained behind, a somewhat unwelcome bequest to the widow M'Gurk. Indeed, I fear the creature became a source of some annoyance to her, because Andy Sheridan contracted a habit of addressing it by the name of Tishy, and bestowing upon it the same laudatory epithets with which the widow had been wont to justify her admiration for the energetic sisters.

It was on a hushed February morning that the Patmans finally departed. The smell of spring was in the air, and filmy silvery mist had begun to float off the dark bogland in vanishing wreaths, soft and dim as the frail sloe-blossom already stolen out over the writhen black branches up on the ridge. A jewel had been left in the heart of every groundling trefoil and clover-leaf, and the long rays that twinkled to them were still just tinged with rose. Here and there a flake of gold seemed to have lit upon the clump of sombre green furze-bushes, by which neighbours in a small knot stood watching the three generations of Patmans dwindle away down the road with its narrow dewy grass-border threading the vast sweep of sky-rimmed brown. Father and son walked, while little Katty bobbed along balanced in a swaying donkey-pannier. The widow M'Gurk, who felt a good deal of concern about the destiny of her late lodgers, hoped they were goin' to dacint people, for there wasn't as much sinse among the three of them as you'd put on a fourpenny bit; and Mrs. Quigley thought "'twould be hard to say which, the young man or the ould one, was the foolishest; for the blathers ould Joe talked about Tom, and the gaby Tom made of himself over the child, now that he had his own way wid her, was past belief."

"And I can tell you," said Ody Rafferty, "there's folks goin' about that you'll want all the wits you ever had, and maybe somethin' tacked on, to get the better of rightly."

"Augh, I question will they ever do any great things, goodness help them," said Mrs. Sheridan. "'Twill be much if he keeps them outside the House."

"Well, anyway," said Biddy Ryan, "I'd liefer be in their coats, fortin or no fortin, than like them two ugly-tempered women, settin' off to the dear knows where, after robbin' and plunderin' all before them."

"True for you then, Biddy," said Mrs. Brian, turning away from her wide outlook; "we're none so badly off, when we're stoppin' where we are, instid of streelin' about wid the notion of such villainies in our minds. For sure enough," she said, as she faced round towards the grey-peaked endwalls and russet thatch of Lisconnel, "the world's a quare place to get travellin' through, take it as you will."

www.ingramcontent.com/pod-product-compliance
Lightning Source LLC
Chambersburg PA
CBHW030736230426
43667CB00007B/733